Praise for *Light Is the New Black*

'*Light Is The New Black* is an inspiring book with a message that is so needed right now. Rebecca courageously guides us to turn our lights on and follow the daily calls of our soul so we can all light up the world with our authentic spirit.'
– SONIA CHOQUETTE, BESTSELLING AUTHOR OF *THE ANSWER IS SIMPLE*

'I'm a super-fan of Rebecca Campbell and her new book, *Light Is the New Black*. This book is relatable, real, soul-centered and empowering. Rebecca guides her reader to step into their authentic power so that they can live and lead at their highest potential. *Light Is the New Black* is a must read for all Spirit Junkies on their path to living a miraculous life.'
– GABRIELLE BERNSTEIN, *NEW YORK TIMES* BESTSELLING AUTHOR OF *MIRACLES NOW*

'Prepare to be lit from within, to remember the tremendous levity of the soul, and to return to the limitless home of love and light that is our birthright. *Light Is The New Black* contains the same mystical energy that compelled Rebecca Campbell to write it. It's pure transmission. It's pure memory of our truest purpose while here: be the light. And it's a pragmatic, spiritual guide for being the light right now – right in the midst of our messy, everyday lives.'
– MEGGAN WATTERSON, AUTHOR OF *REVEAL* AND *HOW TO LOVE YOURSELF (AND SOMETIMES OTHER PEOPLE)*

'Rebecca Campbell is a modern day High Priestess led by the Divine. I've never in my life met anyone who shines like she does. Rebecca is the real deal. Bringing clarity to the deepest of spiritual subjects, this book is a response to the call of the soul. Will you step up? It's your time to shine! We are born with light – it's within us right now, but the busy world can make us forget. Through *Light Is the New Black*, let Rebecca lead you back the source of light so you can share it with the world and live a life that's filled with soul and purpose.'
– KYLE GRAY, AUTHOR OF *WINGS OF FORGIVENESS*

'Each new generation needs a new inspirational voice. To me, Rebecca Campbell is that voice. I just love witnessing a new, young talent about to unleash a storm that will change the way we think about our personal empowerment and spirituality.'
– MEL CARLILE, MANAGIN'

'Rebecca Campbell ... ... ew wave of vibrant visionaries to emerg ... . Part memoir and part guidebook, *Ligh* ...) follow her heart, feed her spirit and al ...
– NANCY LEVIN, BESTSELLING ... ... OF *JUMP... AND YOUR LIFE WILL APPEAR*

'Rebecca is authentic, empowered and beautifully honest in her writing and as a person. This book is soul treasure; drink in her wisdom and let it light your way to a deeper experience of your true self and your divine purpose.'
– HOLLIE HOLDEN

'In order to light up the world and throw our arms around our most authentic selves, we need to ask questions, and then, oh boy, do we need to listen. *Light Is the New Black* is for the real you. Raw, honest, and heart achingly bright, Rebecca's words hone directly in on the lost knowledge that you have deep inside. In one invigorating swoop, her gentle wisdom and straight-to-the-core practical tools guide you to reignite your inner pilot light. There is no going back now; this book is your golden wake-up call and the ultimate Q & A for your soul.'
– LOUISE ANDROLIA, ARTIST, INTUITIVE, EMPOWERMENT COACH, AND MAGIC MAKER

'In *Light Is the New Black*, Rebecca Campbell shares a great truth, a "secret" that most of us don't discover until much later in life, if ever. Our light comes from within, and when life conspires to turn out that light we must find it for ourselves, within ourselves. You'll love taking this inspiring journey with Rebecca to reconnect with your own light, turn it on, and illuminate the path to your soul's calling. Once you do, everything in your life reflects back that light as you express the truth of who you really are.'
– GAIL LARSEN, FOUNDER OF REAL SPEAKING® AND AUTHOR OF *TRANSFORMATIONAL SPEAKING: IF YOU WANT TO CHANGE THE WORLD, TELL A BETTER STORY*

'The Divine has found a beautiful voice in Rebecca's new book, *Light Is the New Black*. What lies between these pages cracked me open and reminded me that I'm no longer alone. Written with a big, open heart and a fierce commitment to sharing the truth, Rebecca's spiritual journey will inspire you to turn on your light and shine it bright.'
– LISA LISTER, AUTHOR OF *CODE RED: KNOW YOUR FLOW, UNLOCK YOUR MONTHLY SUPER POWERS & CREATE A BLOODY AMAZING LIFE. PERIOD.*

'Rebecca is a vibrant and authentic voice in the emerging self-empowerment landscape, and effortlessly marries the numinous call of the soul with real-life wisdom for women on the rise. *Light Is the New Black* is a call to arms for the next generation of spiritual seekers to get switched on to their true path, and make each minute of this life really count!'
– RUBY WARRINGTON, FOUNDER OF THENUMINOUS.NET

'Rebecca's new book is as soulful and light-filled as she is. If you have a burning desire to discover yourself, answer the callings of your soul, and live a marvelous life, look no further! *Light Is the New Black* is a must read for every Modern Mystic who wants to create magic, work their inner light, and burst its unique brightness onto the world.'
– BELINDA DAVIDSON, MEDICAL INTUITIVE, SPIRITUAL MENTOR, AND FOUNDER OF SCHOOL OF THE MODERN MYSTIC

LIGHT

IS THE NEW BLACK

LIGHT

IS THE NEW BLACK

A Guide to Answering your SOUL'S CALLINGS
and WORKING YOUR LIGHT

REBECCA CAMPBELL

HAY HOUSE

Carlsbad, California • New York City • London • Sydney
Johannesburg • Vancouver • Hong Kong • New Delhi

FOR BLAIR, WHO NEVER DIMMED HIS LIGHT.

LET NOTHING DIM
THE LIGHT THAT
SHINES WITHIN.

MAYA ANGELOU

First published and distributed in the United Kingdom by:
Hay House UK Ltd, Astley House, 33 Notting Hill Gate, London W11 3JQ
Tel: +44 (0)20 3675 2450; Fax: +44 (0)20 3675 2451; www.hayhouse.co.uk

Published and distributed in the United States of America by:
Hay House Inc., PO Box 5100, Carlsbad, CA 92018-5100
Tel: (1) 760 431 7695 or (800) 654 5126
Fax: (1) 760 431 6948 or (800) 650 5115; www.hayhouse.com

Published and distributed in Australia by:
Hay House Australia Ltd, 18/36 Ralph St, Alexandria NSW 2015
Tel: (61) 2 9669 4299; Fax: (61) 2 9669 4144; www.hayhouse.com.au

Published and distributed in the Republic of South Africa by:
Hay House SA (Pty) Ltd, PO Box 990, Witkoppen 2068
info@hayhouse.co.za

Published and distributed in India by:
Hay House Publishers India, Muskaan Complex, Plot No.3, B-2,
Vasant Kunj, New Delhi 110 070
Tel: (91) 11 4176 1620; Fax: (91) 11 4176 1630; www.hayhouse.co.in

Distributed in Canada by:
Raincoast Books, 2440 Viking Way, Richmond, B.C. V6V 1N2
Tel: (1) 604 448 7100; Fax: (1) 604 270 7161; www.raincoast.com

A catalogue record for this book is available from the British Library.

ISBN: 978-1-78180-501-5

Song lyrics p.11 © Gurunam Singh, devotional singer/Naad yoga teacher (gurunamsingh.com)

Printed and bound by CPI Group (UK) Ltd, Croydon, CR0 4YY

△
CONTENTS

Part III – Work Your Light

△

FROM THE UNIVERSE TO ME TO YOU

Listening is one thing; acting on what you hear is another. When I first woke up to the callings of my soul, I lacked the courage, confidence, inner support, and practical tools not to hear the callings of my soul but to let them truly lead my life. There were pieces missing, a journey needed to be taken. I called upon the Universe and spiritual teachers to support me. This book is the result of that journey.

You can read it in one sitting, one chapter a day or pick a page at random for an instant hit of guidance. Throughout you will find 'Work Your Light' exercises, mantras, and affirmations. I created these with the intention of guiding you not only to *hear* the callings of your soul, but to *act* on them too.

While I was there for the writing of these pages, I cannot take credit for them all. They are a combination: one girl's journey (that'd be mine); channeled messages from the Universe and the Councils of Light; lessons learned from my teachers; and the poems, prayers, and words of encouragement that I needed most.

There is no one word that captures the magnificent, illuminating presence that connects us all. However, in an attempt to do so, I have used the terms Source, the Universe, Light, God, and Grace. If the particular word I have used doesn't resonate with you, just trade it for one that feels right.

Also mentioned is the term 'Lightworker,' by which I mean someone who consciously chooses to answer the call of spirit/soul/Source/the light over the call of the ego/fear/control/darkness. Just by reading this book, you are working your light. Thank you for working your light.

I pray that you experience a sense of remembering of the beautiful being that you already are and were always destined to be.

I pray that you never feel alone, that you always find the light nestled just behind the shadows, and the courage to act on the gentle, constant callings of your soul.

I pray that you find the inspiration, courage, confidence, inner support, and practical tools not only to act on the unique callings of your soul, but to let them lead your life.

I pray that you discover the authentic gift to the world that you already are and choose to serve the world by being You.

The world doesn't just need light; it needs your unique light.

So much love,

Rebecca x

THE WORLD WILL BE SAVED BY THE WESTERN WOMAN.

THE DALAI LAMA

△

INTRODUCTION

'Never doubt that a small group of thoughtful,
committed citizens can change the world;
indeed, it's the only thing that ever has.'
MARGARET MEAD

At the Peace Conference in Canada in 2009, the Dalai Lama said, 'The world will be saved by the Western woman,' and it was a call to action for women throughout the West. This book is a response to that call.

It's a book for a new breed of women and men who are here to be bright lights in the world: modern-day Lightworkers, who agreed at a soul level to be here at this time in history, to bring us into the Age of Light (led by spirit and Divine Feminine). I know because I'm one of them and I know I am not alone.

This time we are living in right now has been prophesied by the mystics and sages of all the ages. It is an era in history in which we are all being called to embrace our truest, brightest, most authentic selves and rise up.

In order to succeed in the Age of Light, everything in our lives must be an authentic expression of who we truly are. There is a global shift occurring where inauthenticity no longer stands a chance. Relationships, jobs, brands, or anything that is not in alignment with the flow of the Universe (and who we truly are) is becoming harder to hold on to. It's as though our inner and outer foundations are crumbling away, in an effort to reconnect us with the authentic light within, so we can get back in flow with the Universe. And the falling apart will not let up until our inner and outer worlds are aligned.

Seemingly overnight, my whole life came crumbling down. No matter how hard I tried to hold it all together, anything that was based on fear, neediness, force, control, or inauthenticity was unable to survive.

For too long we have been living in a patriarchal society, where the ego-driven powers of fear, unconsciousness, separateness, and control have been at the forefront. During this time there have been amazing advances in technology, standards of living, and education, yet we are more depressed and lonelier than ever.

Moving out of patriarchy is not about the feminine ruling over the masculine, rather a more balanced state of being where we embrace the authenticity of who we are and realize that we are all connected, part of a larger whole. The rising feminine can be found in both men and women. Therefore, when I mention 'she' or 'sister,' I am speaking to the compassionate, protective, intuitive, and conscious feminine that is rapidly awakening and inviting that part of us to rise up.

With the planet in the state that it is, we cannot continue the way we have been. Mother Earth is calling forth a new awakening of consciousness in order for us to survive on this magnificent planet we call home. A shift from aggression to compassion, from fact to truth, from fear to love, from separateness to oneness, from unquestioned dogma to faith, from left brain to right, from war to peace, from force to flow, from unconsciousness to consciousness, and from unquestioned linear processes to lateral solutions.

We each have a light within us waiting to guide us home. Our Soul Purpose is to shine this unique light in a way that only we can. In doing so, we spark something in another and inspire them to do the same.

We are all being called to align our lives and answer the deep stirrings of our souls. I believe that through doing so, we can move into a new stage of Earth's history. It is a time when masculine and feminine energies swing back into balance, and when we acknowledge the inter-connectedness of all living beings.

As each one of us lights up, we will effortlessly spark something in another, and rise up together.

I believe that we can change the world, one conscious, authentic person at a time.

And I believe that you are here to lead the way.

Rise sister rise.

△
RISE SISTER RISE

When your plans and schemes and your hopes
and dreams beg for you to let them go.

Rise sister rise.

When the life you have so consciously
created all comes crumbling down.

Rise sister rise.

When your soul is heavy and your heart broken in two.

Rise sister rise.

When you gave it your best, and it wasn't quite enough.

Rise sister rise.

When you've been beaten and defeated,
and feel so far away from home.

Rise sister rise.

When you find yourself in a thousand pieces,
with no idea which bit goes where.

Rise sister rise.

When you have loved and lost. And then lost again.

Rise sister rise.

When your wings have been clipped, spirit

dampened, and all you hear is a whisper.

Rise sister rise.

When you finally beg mercy to your calling
but have no idea where to start.

Rise sister rise.

Rise for you. And rise for me.

For when you rise first you make the path brighter for She.

△

BASK IN THE LIGHT

I'm devoted to doing all I can to support your rising. My vision for *Light Is the New Black* has always been more than just these pages. Below are some ways that you can bask in the light some more while you read.

www.LightIsTheNewBlack.com

Get over to www.lightisthenewblack.com for free meditations, tools, interviews and gifts.

#LightIsTheNewBlack

Share the light while you read using #LightIsTheNewBlack.

Light Sourcing

Throughout this book I reference my Light Sourcing meditation. If you want to create huge shifts in your life, you can download it for free (*yay!*) at www.lightisthenewblack.com. Try it for 21 days and watch the Universe bend towards you.

Light Is The New Black Spotify Soundtrack

Get some light for your ears by listening along to the free playlist while you read at www.lightisthenewblack.com

Part I

LOSING EVERYTHING FINDING ME

One girl's journey

Δ

CALL OFF THE SEARCH PARTY,
I WAS INSIDE ME ALL ALONG

We all have an inner light waiting to guide us home. But sometimes the Universe turns off all the lights, so we have no choice but to find our own. Perhaps that's been the case for you; it certainly has been for me.

For as long as I can remember, I had this inner knowing that I was here for a reason. I knew I had a purpose, a calling, but the whole thing stressed me out. It was like walking around with this huge weight of responsibility on my shoulders. It felt like I had this urgent thing to do and time was running out.

You know that feeling when you have an assignment or work to do on the weekend, and you can't relax until it's done?

Well, I had that feeling constantly. As if there was something that I was forgetting, a whisper that I couldn't quite make out. The feeling niggled me: there when I went to bed; there in the middle of the night; and there when I woke up in the morning.

I'd spent the majority of my life looking outside of myself for answers. Reaching for anything I could get my hands on, in order to soothe the subtle aching, longing, yearning, and calling deep within my soul, which said that there was something I was missing. There was something more.

I turned to relationships, career, travel, food, alcohol, and partying, but none of them quite hit the spot. I tried traveling to the ends of the planet, in search for something that I couldn't quite put my finger on...

I was pushing, striving, and controlling, instead of listening, trusting, and allowing. It took my whole life to come tumbling down for me to realize that everything I was searching for was inside me all along.

My soul was always calling. I was just facing the wrong way.

△

WHAT I THOUGHT WAS ROCK BOTTOM

By the time 2011 came along, it felt like my life was held together by a single thread, and at any moment the whole tower would come crashing down.

Originally from Australia, I'd just achieved my long-term career ambition of becoming the creative director of a London advertising agency by the age of 30. But the moment I got it, I felt nothing. Isn't this what I had worked so hard for? Why I had sacrificed so much? Overnight I knew that my career no longer fitted my soul.

My relationship of over 10 years was on its last legs, but I refused to admit it. Matt and I had met at university. Creative, sensitive, and hilarious, his cool nonchalance was ridiculously attractive and I fell for him immediately.

The first couple of years were wonderful, but as time went on we became more and more entangled, and more and more stuck. Matt had been suffering from chronic depression for several years. Living in London, far away from the support of our respective families, we ignored the reality of the situation.

I refused to admit that things were broken, throwing myself into a million-and-one ways to fix it, rather than surrender and accept. My gift of seeing the potential in people wasn't serving either of us one bit.

The worse everything seemed to get, the harder I tried to hold it all together. The harder I tried to hold it all together, the more I ignored the callings of my soul. The more I ignored the callings of my soul, the more out of flow with the Universe I got. The more out of flow with the Universe I got, the more alone I felt.

I hadn't felt real joy in my heart for years, but the thought of not being with Matt was too hard to bear. We loved each other with every ounce of our hearts, but in truth we had become best friends more than life partners. With every day, I felt more trapped and stuck in a life that I had worked so hard to create. The thought of saying goodbye to the one person who had been by my side through my entire adult life was too hard to comprehend. I was petrified of being alone and of nothing coming in to take its place.

My external world wasn't in alignment with my internal one. I was way out of flow with the Universe. I knew my soul was calling me to make a massive career change – to follow my passion for spiritual development, intuition, and the journey of the soul. But I was petrified of coming out of the spiritual closet, and turning my back on the great career and network I had worked so hard to create.

I began waking up at 3.13 a.m. each night, drenched in sweat, unable to catch my breath. Alone in bed, I could hear Matt down the hall still on his computer. My loneliness was palpable. Sometimes I would get onto my hands and knees and just sob, begging God to miraculously get me out of there because I lacked the courage to do it myself.

△

CRACKED OPEN

On April 15, 2011, I woke up to the news that Blair, one of my very best friends, had been diagnosed with acute myeloid leukemia. My heart fell through the bed, in a desperate attempt to get back to Australia. Blair held a part of my soul that no one else on the planet did. With him I could let my entire truest, biggest, most authentic self shine. He knew my secret dreams and held similar ones.

The moment we met it was an instant soul connection. I loved him immediately. Blair had a contagious charisma and he completely owned it. He wasn't afraid of being his biggest self and encouraged others to do the same: A lover of life, an exceptional human, and king of good times.

Blair was the only person my own age with whom I could talk candidly about my spiritual life. The first night we met, we discovered we were both reading the same book, Doreen Virtue's *The Lightworker's Way*. We planned to write books and 'change the world' together. But first we would become successful in our chosen fields (him as an actor and me as a creative director), and *then* we would use our power to change the world.

As the day progressed Blair's condition worsened. I prayed for a sign as to whether or not I should fly back to Australia. Two minutes later, as I was getting something out of my wardrobe, the whole thing fell flat to the floor, emptying out every single item of clothing in front of me. I took it as a sign and got on the next flight.

By the time I was on the plane, Blair's condition had rapidly declined and he was in a medically induced coma. During that long flight home, somewhere over Europe and the Middle East, I physically felt Blair's presence. I could feel the actual weight of his body pressing down on mine. I could smell his aftershave and the warmth of his lips kissing my forehead. His hand pressed down on my chest, soothing my aching heart. And in that moment, I knew he was gone.

Years earlier, we had made a pact that whoever died first had to visit the other immediately, so we knew they were OK and hanging out in the afterlife.

For someone relatively young, I had experienced a fair amount of death. But this was different. Blair was different. This was not part of the plan.

I fell into a deep, dark, regretful place, which no one could carry me out of.

▽

A couple of months later we suddenly lost another dear friend from the same tightly knit friendship circle.

The Universe was not letting up.

I felt cheated, bitter and mad. I had no fight left. I wanted a refund from God.

Despite Matt and I supporting each other through the grief of losing our friends, one Sunday in October after celebrating my 30th birthday, we agreed to end our relationship. And before I knew it, I was watching a black cab disappear into the distance, taking away the person I had spent my whole adult life with – down the street to the other side of the globe and out of my life.

Winter was coming. I was alone, unreachable, and a long way from home.

△

FOUNDATIONS COME CRUMBLING

The only thing that got me through the months that followed was the work ethic my parents had instilled in me. I chose them well.

The grief would hit out of nowhere: at my desk, on the subway, in the grocery store aisle, while walking down the street.

My family and friends urged me to come back home to Australia, but deep down I had this inner knowing that this was something I needed to face alone. I needed to venture into the darkest caverns and try to find my own way out.

In an attempt to create a clean slate for myself, I moved into a studio apartment in the heart of London's Notting Hill. Within a week I discovered even that was falling apart. The foundations of the building were literally crumbling around me.

All the structures that stood before me had to be replaced. The irony was not lost on me. The world was my mirror.

One particular night it all got too much and I was near giving up. As tears streamed uncontrollably down my face, the water pipes exploded in unison, transforming my home into a stinking sea of watery despair.

Seriously Universe?

I found myself on the water-soaked carpet in complete surrender, praying (more like begging) for mercy. It wasn't the slightest bit graceful, and went something like this:

'God... Please help.

Please God help.

Seriously, I give up.

I GIVE UP.

I F*ING GIVE UP.

For F's sake I don't know what the F you want me to do.

I can't F*ing do this anymore.

PLEASE GOD F*ING HELP ME!

WHAT THE HELL DO YOU WANT ME TO DO?'

Then all of a sudden, I clearly heard the words, *Go to Chicago*.

Followed by a feeling of ultimate calm and relief.

I was like, 'Chicago? WTF is in Chicago?'

I racked my brains and the only person I knew in Chicago was my teacher Sonia Choquette whom I'd been training with in London for the past four years. Without giving my head a moment to butt in, I immediately looked up her website and emailed her assistant. He replied instantly saying there was a private teacher training in Chicago in a week's time. It was not available to the public, but there was one spot left and Sonia was happy for me to take it.

My mind said, *You've got a huge campaign launching in 14 days at work. You have no vacation left. Your house is falling apart. You are an emotional wreck – do you really want to let people see that? Pfffft teacher? Who do you think you are, training to be a spiritual teacher when you can't even get your life together?*

My soul whispered, *Go to Chicago*.

I knew my life wasn't worth living, unless something changed, so I asked, 'If I am really meant to go, prove it to me and prove it to me good.'

I turned off the water supply, sent a text to my landlord, changed my soaked pajamas, and went back to my semi-floating bed.

The next morning I woke up to a message from my landlord telling me that he'd found someone to fix the apartment, but I would have to move out for a week (*starting the date of the training in Chicago*). He apologized profusely and said I didn't need to pay rent for the next month (*the cost of the tuition and flight*), and he would pay for a hotel of my choice where I could stay while the work was getting done (*the cost of my hotel in Chicago*).

Well done, Universe!

But I still had a whopping big campaign launching...

An hour later, I arrived at work to discover the campaign had been delayed due to a PR scandal. And get this: The CEO then suggested that I take some time off while things were quiet, as I would need to be on standby after the PR scandal had died down in a month or so.

Well bloody done, Universe!

I took the blatant hint, booked my flight immediately, and for the first time in a long time, stepped onto the magic carpet and trusted the ride.

△
FINDING GRACE

From the moment I walked onto the plane, to sitting in front of the fire in Chicago drying out my waterlogged heart, I felt as though I was in exactly the right place. I could feel Blair cheering me on. It was like I was the main character of a movie that I had seen before. Déjà vu on steroids. As if I was being cradled by life. I slept the whole night through for the first time in forever and, while my heart was still heavy, I woke with a new light of hope.

The next evening, after a long day, I found myself sitting in front of devotional singer Gurunam Singh, and his seriously sexy drummer, Chris Maguire, who were there to play for us.

Having listened to a few songs and joined in with the chanting, my heart opened some more, and through the cracks my soul sheepishly edged forward. Gurunam's eyes caught mine and I could feel him holding my soul. I was about to have the most extreme healing of my life. (Go to www.lightisthenewblack.com to download this grace-filled song.) He sang:

Give up all your hopes and your dreams.
Give up all your plans and your schemes.
Give up the fear of darkness surrounded in the light.
Give up fear of being wrong and the need to be right.
Unto thee, unto thee, unto thee, unto thee.
Unto thee, unto thee, unto thee, unto thee.
Unto thee, unto thee, unto thee, unto thee.
I give everything I am... unto thee.

In that moment, I realized how much time I had wasted trying to control and force my life. I was absolutely exhausted from desperately trying to hold it all together for so long. I had no fight left and it was time to let go of the reins.

As Gurunam continued to sing, I mourned the loss of Blair. I grieved for the end of my relationship with Matt, the family that would never be, and the daughter I hadn't met (I'd had a miscarriage a year earlier). I cried for my inner voice that I had ignored for so long. I cried for all of the years I had spent in my masculine – pushing and striving instead of letting life support me. I wept for the exuberant woman inside me who longed to emerge. I mourned for all the time I had spent searching for things outside of myself, when really the only place I needed to look was within. I sobbed for the light deep within my heart, which no matter how hard I'd tried to snuff out, still shone bright.

Past, present, but mostly future, I mourned for it all. And during those 3 minutes and 39 seconds, my ego finally surrendered and asked my soul to lead.

In that short moment, I touched a space within me that can only be described as Grace. I surrendered. I touched God; or rather I received God to touching me. I came home. I realized that while I felt separate, I was actually part of a greater whole, or oneness, and thus never really separate or alone.

I realized the only reason I felt unsupported was because I wasn't supporting myself. The only reason I felt alone was because I had ignored the callings of my soul. And for the first time I was able to see beyond the devastation and truly feel the bountiful light of Grace.

I was learning, and yet also remembering who I truly was. Like the depths of me who already knew were saying, *Yes, yes, this way.*

I experienced a coming home to my authentic self, different from ever before, and felt my soul cheer.

While Gurunam sang his next song, *The Grace of God*, I had this big fat whopping mother of an 'aha' light-bulb moment, where I finally understood what I had been searching for all this time.

My entire life I'd had this weird fascination with a thing called 'nominative determinism' – when people's names fit their calling or purpose in life, like little clues from the heavens. For example, William Wordsworth was a writer, Larry Speakes is a White House speaker, Tracey Cox is a sex therapist, and Lisa Messenger is the founder of Collective Magazine. But I'd always felt a bit cheated by my name. In Hebrew, Rebecca means 'knotted cord,' or 'to bind.'

I didn't want to be a basket and I certainly didn't want to be a knotted cord. Then it hit me. Up until this point, I had spent my whole life searching for meaning, trying to unbind myself from the knotted bundle of thoughts that makes me, Me.

My last name, Campbell, is Scottish for 'crooked mouth' – inauthenticity at its best – which considering how long I had been ignoring my inner voice and hiding out in my spiritual closet, was pretty fitting. But then, right smack bang in the center of it all was my middle name... Grace.

Without even realizing it, Grace was the exact thing I had been searching for my entire life. And she was right there inside me all along. Searching north, south, east, and west trying to control, force and make it happen, when all I really needed to do was surrender to the gentle callings of my soul and allow the light of Grace to guide me.

△

LIVING IN THE LIGHT

My inner light was burning bright. I was home. Now that I had found it, there was no way I was going to let it go. I vowed to say 'YES' to every little call from my soul, regardless of how much logical sense it made. I vowed to do everything I could never to turn my back on myself again.

Just as the old saying goes, 'When the student is ready the teacher will appear,' the very next day I was taught a form of meditation known as 'Sourcing' (which I'll share with you on page 182 and you can download at www.lightisthenewblack.com). Using this simple tool, I was able to fill myself up with Source energy (of which we are all a part), rather than turning to anything outside of myself.

I started Sourcing and listening to the callings of my soul every day without fail. I made it a non-negotiable part of my life.

I showed up every day.

Within a few months, my life was unrecognizable. I felt supported because I was supporting myself. My soul was content because I was acting on its callings. My foundations became strong because I was fuelling myself from within. Through the daily act of letting go, receiving, and allowing myself to be supported I was able to heal my aching heart and let my inner light lead the way.

I continued excavating my life, only letting the things that served me stay.

Alignment was key.

Replacing 'should' and 'could' with deep desires and 'why not?' I danced, breathed, shook off, and embraced. I only let in people, experiences, and things that filled me up, lit me up, and made me feel whole.

Consciously choosing not to enter a relationship until I was completely healed and whole, I discovered that I did not need someone else to be IN love. Instead it was possible to be IN LOVE (in the flow of love) all on my own.

By filling up myself first, I found I was able to show up to my relationships brighter and more whole than ever. Layer by layer, I allowed myself to get authentically naked and come out of the spiritual closet for real.

I quit my corporate job and my intuitive, spiritual mentoring practice took off, and my friend Robyn Silverton and I co-founded The Spirited Project and started teaching Spirited Sessions every month. New people (my kind of people) started arriving serendipitously on my doorstep.

Then I met someone who had been on his own journey home and I invited him to be in love (a space of love) with me. I don't *need* him in my life, but I sure as hell want and love him in it. Last September he asked me to marry him and I said a big fat YES.

My prayers were answered beyond anything that I could have imagined. All I ever needed to do was surrender and let my soul courageously lead.

Call off the search party. I was inside me all along.

△
WAKING UP

Rewind to the nineties.

Every now and then, the Universe conspires to cross our path with someone in a way that feels like they were put on this planet just for us. Had a particular meeting not taken place, perhaps you would have remained asleep? That was certainly the case the day I met Angela Wood.

Soon after starting high school aged 14, I began experiencing what I can only describe now as my first awakening. A natural empath, I would pass strangers on the street and feel their innermost thoughts and feelings.

All of this cracked wide open after I read an article in *Dolly* magazine about a teenage girl called Anna Wood who tragically died after taking the drug ecstasy. In the interview Anna's mother, Angela, openly shared the loss of her beautiful bright light of a daughter. This article touched my soul so deeply, and I remember sobbing myself to sleep from the sadness I felt for Anna's mother without really knowing why or being able to express my thoughts.

The next day I got the bus to the bookshop and bought *Anna's Story*, the biography of Anna Wood's life. The following day at school, I began passionately telling my friend how much Anna's story had touched my heart.

I turned to the page of the book where there was a picture of Anna and her mother and said, 'It's really weird, I can't explain why, but I just have this urge to find Angela and give her the hugest hug, and try to take away some of her pain.'

My friend said, 'That *is* really weird.' She then looked up, back down to the book and then back up again, and pointed, saying: 'That lady over there kinda looks like Anna's mother.'

I looked up at a tall blonde woman making her way across the school courtyard, and realized... IT WAS HER! It was Angela Wood!

I hesitated for a moment, unable to get my head around the weird serendipity of it all, but then, moved by a force bigger than my mind or body, I found myself running after her. The school vice Principal intercepted me with a question and mid-sentence, I turned back around to find that Angela was nowhere to be seen. Heart deflated I finished the conversation. As I turned around to head back to my friends, I found Anna's mum, Angela Wood, looking back at me.

Everything seemed to stand still and we had this weird moment of deep soul recognition... before I introduced myself and bumbled about doing my best to express how much her story impacted me, clutching the book in my hand. Angela then invited me to attend her talk that she was about to give to the senior year. Knowing I must be there, I skipped math and sneaked into Angela's talk – doing my best not to stand out. Afterwards, I waited sheepishly to talk to her and we made plans to stay in contact.

Angela later told me that it was her birthday the week we met. That morning she had asked Anna for a birthday present, and she knew our meeting was it.

We quickly became friends. Our families met and were generously understanding of our seemingly odd relationship.

We'd spend hours sipping coffee and deep in conversation about the meaning of life, the afterlife, grief, death, past lives, and angels. We'd trade dreams, poetry, books, and theories on life and the Universe. I learned firsthand about the power of the human heart and the courage of the human spirit. I'd listen for hour upon hour as Angela shared her stories about the life and death of her beautiful bright light of a daughter Anna. How she touched people's hearts more deeply in her 15 short years than most do in 80.

I pray to be able to do the same.

During those years I found myself getting off the school bus and walking up the steep hill in a sort of creative trance, words rushing through me that I had to get down. They would flow from my soul without effort and with a feeling of grace. I'd write about what was happening with the world, what happens when you die, that our loved ones lost never really leave us, and how we each have our own team of angels and spirit guides around us. Often I would wake the next morning not remembering what I had created.

Looking back, I see now that I was channeling – although, perhaps, all creativity is just that. Messages and ideas that are waiting to be born to people who are open enough to receive them.

During school vacations I would sometimes join Angela on the road at her speaking events as she spoke about how precious life is, how we must hold those we care about and tell them how much we love them. I watched in admiration as her message so effortlessly flowed from her heart.

I pray that one day I might do the same.

I'd been cracked open and all the other things in my life just didn't seem to matter. I'd spend all of my free time and money from my part-time jobs learning about the afterlife, Soul Purpose, past life regression, crystals, healing, and anything I could get my hands on. And all the time it was as if I were remembering things that were deeply engrained in my soul.

Desperately longing to meet other people who thought like me, I'd take two buses and a train to the other side of Sydney to have sessions with healers and psychics, inhaling it all with expanding pleasure. My appetite was insatiable. As I flicked through the pages and listened to the teachers, I experienced what could only be explained as a sense of remembering and homecoming. It felt as though I had found my calling and my true self. Yet, the more connected I felt on the inside, the more isolated I felt on the outside.

A few years later, just after I'd finished high school, Angela moved to the UK. I was devastated and felt like I lost the only person in my life that truly saw the real depths of me. At that stage she was.

I deeply longed to be surrounded by people my own age with whom I could share my innermost thoughts. I felt lost between two worlds – that of being a normal teenager and the expanding world of soul and spirit.

Even then I knew that I wanted to write books and create things to help people heal, but what could a young girl possibly know about healing people when she hadn't had anything significant to heal from herself?

So every night I would pray to God that something really bad would happen to me, so I had an external reason to feel all the things I was feeling and so I could help other people's hearts and souls – as I felt called to do. I figured if I had been through enough tragedy myself, then at least I could write about that. I'd wake up each day, wondering when the tragedy would hit. But it never did. Life was 'good' and I felt more alone than ever. So I ignored the callings of my soul and decided to dim to fit in.

I consciously went into what I now call my 'spiritual closet,' keeping my metaphysical studies a secret. I waited for the day when I would be justified to speak of the things that dwelled deep within me. Until that day came, I was determined to keep it all inside.

△

'F YOU GOD'

Fast forward to 2012.

Six months after returning from my grace-filled experience in Chicago I knew I needed to heal the lingering pieces of grief that remained, and my soul called me to go on silent retreat in Assisi with my friend Robyn.

We spent the mornings and evenings deep in meditation while our days were given over to walking the wildflower-filled trail of St. Francis, church hopping, and gorging on orgasmic Italian food – well, it would have been rude not to.

After meditation on the third night I was overcome with this unexpected and unrecognizable red-hot rage bubbling up from the depths of my core. Unable to talk (very frustrating!) I grabbed my Moleskine and headed for the hills.

On a bench in the middle of a field under a swollen Virgo moon, I started writing furiously what turned out to be a hate letter to God.

Through desperate sobs I let it all out. I ranted and raved to God, demanding to know, *What have I done to deserve all of this? Why no matter how hard I've tried to hold everything together and do the right thing, still nothing has worked out... Why do you expect me to believe in you, if you don't even have the balls to show your face?*

I was pissed off. Big time. Ever since I was a little girl I had this unwavering knowing that God/the Universe existed. And so, for a 'believer' I felt totally ripped off and unsupported. I held nothing back. Through angry sobs I ranted on for pages with my pen, at times piercing through to the next page.

When I had finally got it all out, I felt an overwhelming sense of calm and my sobbing ceased. All of a sudden, the energy around me shifted and I watched as my hand started moving on its own accord. As my hand moved across the page, I realized that God was writing her response.

You asked for this, don't you remember?

You said you weren't ready to answer your calling until you had some life experiences.

Well, you have your lessons and your stories, just like you asked.

Now, Rebecca, it's time to get to work.

In an instant I recalled all those pleas I'd made when I was younger. I understood that my suffering didn't happen *TO* me, it happened *FOR* me. I took a deep breath, gathered my notebook and marched myself back to my room.

I was ready.

Finally I was ready.

Tucked into bed, gazing out my window at the star-filled night sky, knowing that tomorrow was going to be a very new day.

I started writing this book the next day.

Part II

TURN YOUR LIGHT ON

Coming home to yourself

YOU WANDER FROM ROOM TO ROOM. HUNTING FOR THE DIAMOND NECKLACE. THAT IS ALREADY AROUND YOUR NECK.

RUMI

△

REMEMBERING

I believe that everyone has a calling and that deep down we all know why we are here. We might not consciously remember it, but our soul does. And every second of every day it's doing its best to call us towards it.

As our life unfolds bit by bit, our memory is sparked and we experience moments of *Ooh, this is familiar*, or *I feel drawn to do more of this*, or *I wish I could spend my life doing this*. It's almost as if we have been here before or have seen this part of the movie. Our soul might give us clues through our excitement or enthusiasm. Little butterflies in our stomach or an extra push towards something.

These little signs are always happening, but they are easy to miss. Our mind doesn't trust them, thinking that it needs to be much more complicated than simply following what lights us up.

In 2008, during a past-life regression session, I was taken back to the moment before this life where I received my own personal mission from the Councils of Light. I was taken to a massive, open, very bright, and white space where many other souls were gathering too. While I could not see other 'people,' I could see and feel their energy as balls of buzzing, glowing white light. It was hard to differentiate where one soul started and another began. It was like the best reunion you could possibly imagine. The atmosphere was electric – buzzing with total anticipation – like just before a Beyoncé, Kylie, or Lady Gaga concert. Some of the different souls' energies were familiar, as if I had incarnated with a few of them before.

As a group we were then given our brief for this lifetime on Earth. We were informed that in this incarnation we would use the interconnectedness of new media and communication to create a mass spiritual awakening in the Western world. Many of us would begin our careers in different fields of media where we would learn the skills to speak out, forming a sort of supportive sisterhood amongst like-hearted women and men – moved by Divine Feminine.

We were told that our missions would be deeply infused in us and we would be sent people and situations that would wake us up from our slumber early in life. As one of us woke up and chose to step out and work our light, it would spark a deep-seeded memory in another, regardless of how physically close we were to each other.

Once we were awake, it would change something in us and we were to follow what lit us up and, in doing so, light up the world around us. As we would do this, it would cause a chain reaction of mass-awakening. We all then received information on our choice of life and our own personal missions.

I couldn't tell you if there were 100 or 100,000 souls there with me, because in truth it felt like we were all one – which of course we were (and we are) – one big Army of Light. If you're reading this, perhaps you were there too?

WORK YOUR LIGHT

What does your soul want you to remember?

WELCOME TO THE AGE OF LIGHT

Welcome to the Age of Light

(It's safe to shine now.)

Can you imagine a part of you that yearns bravely to shine big and bright?

A part of you, which doesn't let fear override and knows exactly what it is here for?

A part of you that is so ready to step forward, to take the lead, to let itself be fully seen? Like really seen?

A part of you that is ready to stop striving and let the Universe support you wholly?

There's a unique spark within you, a spectrum so big and bright. An ultraviolet fire that has been pushed down, dismissed, abandoned, silenced, rejected. But still it burns.

With every new day, as we each light up, we leave the Dark Ages behind us and leap into the Age of Light. A time in history led by spirit not controlled by ego.

One by one, as we each light up, we remind others that it's safe now.

To come out of hiding. To break the silence.

To shine through the shadows, revealing our inner light in all its authentic glory.

Welcome to the Age of Light.

△

YOU'RE HERE FOR A REASON

Never forget your real identity. You are a luminous cosmic stardust being forged into the crucible of cosmic fire.
Deepak Chopra

We are part of a group of souls who agreed to be here at this time in history: a transition team intended to be beacons of light as we move from the shadow of patriarchy (enslaved by ego) to the Age of Light (lead by Source and Divine Feminine).

You are a highly conscious soul and not all souls on this Earth are. This doesn't mean you are better or worse than anyone else, just a different manifestation of energy and soul history. You may feel lonely at times because deep down you know that not everyone is like you. You may feel isolated because perhaps you hide your truest, biggest, brightest self from the world.

You have worked hard to raise your vibration and now you are being called to truly step into it. You have experienced different worlds than just this one. You have lived in different dimensions and on different planets, and incarnated as different expressions of your true essence. You are both infinite and one.

You are both authentically unique and part of the greater whole.

You are here to remind people that it is OK to be whole. It is OK to shine your light. OK to be unapologetically you. In fact, it's more than OK, it's necessary in order to thrive. But you must go first.

The sooner you step up into the greater most authentic version of You, the sooner your fears will dissipate, the sooner your concerns will begin to fade, the sooner life will bend towards you. The more you will flow with life.

**You are already whole and complete,
why do you resist what you are?**

The more you lean into yourself and spend your time being rather than doing in order to be, the sooner you can be supported beyond your wildest dreams. And you will be supported.

△

YOU ARE LIGHT

Your soul is a unique expression of light from Source, carefully sculpted from your individual experiences from lifetime to lifetime. Arranged together in the most perfect way to make up the magnificent cluster of atoms that is You.

Your body is light too. Every cell in your body emits light every single second. Your unique consciousness emits bio-photons with every thought. No matter which way you look at it you are made of light.

You ARE light.

Shining our light is actually our most natural state. When we are connected to the inner light within us we are connected to the light of the Universe.

There is more than enough room for us all to expand and step into our bigness. We are all notes in the most amazing symphony. We were born to light up and expand together.

When we connect to Source we don't need to rely on any external thing to fill us up. The supply of Source energy (universal light) is unlimited. It never runs out. There is enough for us all. It's where we came from and it's where we will return. When you tap into this infinite power source, you slip into the harmonious flow of the Universe and raise the vibration of the planet. Like the morning sun, when you shine your light, you stir the sleepers and inspire them to wake up too.

I AM LIGHT.

△

YOUR AUTHENTIC SELF IS YOUR LIGHT

There is a shift happening right now where anything inauthentic can no longer survive. The things in our lives that don't serve us are crumbling. Relationships, jobs, social structures, or anything built on shaky ground is destined to tumble down. It's happening to bring us back home to who we truly are, so we can live a life that is in alignment with who we truly are, and who we came here to be. But when you're in the thick of it, it can feel like a personal attack from the Universe.

It seems as though we are being called to ensure that the lives that we build are true reflections of who we are called to be – vibrational matches at soul level. If they aren't, then the foundations will continue to come crashing down until we do.

Our soul is always waiting to guide us. Now more than ever it's so important to tune in and listen to its callings. And it is always calling. To come home to and connect within, rather than looking at people and things outside of us for fulfillment, love, meaning, joy, and to fill the gaping void.

Our authentic self is our light. Our Soul Purpose is to embrace it. But in order to do so it's not just about pretending everything is shiny and bright.

The brightest candle casts the biggest shadow.

Moving through the shadow can be hard, but it's so worth it in the end.

△
YOUR LIGHT IS CONTAGIOUS

You have an inner light within you that is craving to be shared by those around you, by the world at large – but mostly by you.

When you share your unique light, bit by bit, you light up the lives of those around you.

And, one by one, you inspire them to light up too.

It's a chain reaction.

And before long, the whole world lights up.

Your light is contagious.

Δ

WHAT THE *WHAT* IS A LIGHTWORKER?

A Lightworker is anyone who devotes their life to being a bright light in the world. They understand that their actions (no matter how big or small) have the potential to raise the vibration of the planet. A Lightworker soul is awake, conscious that their presence matters, and they are part of something that is bigger than them.

Lightworkers are not just tie-dye-wearing hippies and healers with dreads. Far from it. They are teachers and chefs, writers and singers, producers and cleaners, mothers and mediums, creative directors, and kaftan designers. They're at the country club and the nightclub, in the café and the classroom, the boardroom and the art room.

A Lightworker is someone who makes a conscious decision to answer the call of Source (light) over the call of the ego (fear).

There are two types of energy on this planet: light and dark.

Light energy is unlimited and comes from Source. It's high vibrational, expansive, positive, and full of love. Dark energy is much more dense. It's the manipulation, power struggle and fear. It sees us all as separate, rather than connected spiritual beings. It goes against the flow of the Universe.

Lightworkers turn their light on by following what lights them up and then effortlessly sharing that light with the world around them. They are in tune with the callings of their soul and act on its whispers regardless of fear. They do not need to convince anyone of anything, rather just *be the light.*

While some Lightworkers alive right now incarnated with a conscious mission to be of service (and have been doing so for lifetimes), there are countless souls awakening to the call to be of service.

Anyone who chooses to devote their life to being a bright light in the world IS a Lightworker.

There are no snobby spiritual tests to pass or assignments to hand in. The only requirement is a desire to connect with your own authentic light and a longing to serve their world.

I call it working your light.

Just by reading this book you are working your light. By following what you love, you are working your light. By choosing a higher thought when you find yourself in a bad mood, you are working your light. By encouraging someone instead of criticizing them, you are working your light. By sharing your unique gifts, you are working your light. By connecting to the unlimited supply of love in the Universe, you are working your light. By being true to yourself, you are working your light. By being kind and compassionate, you are working your light.

Definition of a Lightworker: Someone who wholeheartedly makes the decision to make the world a brighter place by being in it. The more conscious we get, the higher our vibration, and the more aligned to Source we become. The more conscious we are, the more we see how everything is connected and how we fit into a larger whole.

Many Lightworkers may find that as they raise their consciousness, they become more energetically sensitive, picking up other people's feelings, energy, and thoughts. You may find it hard to watch the news or violent films. You may also find that any old relationships that are built on manipulation, control, and fear, start to drop away as you are no longer an energetic match to them. In Part III, Living In The Light, you'll find lots of practical tools to protect your energy, and keep you grounded and supported.

For some time now, we have been living in a largely unconscious state. In order for Mother Earth to survive we need a global awakening. This awakening has already begun.

I believe that you are one of souls who chose to lead the way.

△

THE DOUBLE MISSION

Lightworkers have a double mission: To raise their consciousness and the consciousness of the planet.

Lightworker souls who aren't completely awake to this double mission (or calling) can have a niggling feeling that they can't quite shake. An odd inexplicable knowing that there is something that they are forgetting to do and time is running out.

Many Lightworkers are scared of coming out of the 'spiritual closet' and being seen. This may be because in the past (past lives) they have been rejected or punished for speaking their truth and rising up.

Once awake, most Lightworker souls find it hard to have meaningless conversations, jobs, and relationships. It's as if they innately know that there is much more to life and feel the constant nudge to surround them with this 'something more' and get to work. They will remain restless until they step into their calling and follow what lights them up, which is to shine their authentic light in their own unique way.

Many Lightworkers confuse their calling with their job or profession. It's actually much simpler than that. Our soul is always calling.

We follow our calling by following what lights us up.

Before incarnating on this planet you carefully chose your body, family, city, surroundings, and experiences to create a perfect environment. These conditions could have been fortunate or not so fortunate, but whatever they were, they were chosen to give you the perfect experience to eventually light up the world in your own unique way.

Lightworkers are scattered all over the planet in every single corner. Every single one, once awakened, serve the world by being them.

The city where you live, the suffering you've experienced, the education you received, the class system you were born into, the parents who conceived you, and the people who've touched your heart, this, all of this, creates the perfect conditions for you to light up the world around you in a way that only you can.

△

YOUR SOUL PURPOSE

The one thing in life you have to do.
Be the Lighthouse.
YOGI BAJAN

For as long as I can remember, I was in a rush to grow up and get working on my Soul Purpose. When I was little my favorite question was, 'Where are we going today?' Even then I was searching for this thing that I knew I had to find. Eternally looking for the perfect black-and-white answer to the question, 'What is my purpose?'

To be honest, the whole Soul Purpose thing stressed me out. It felt like a big decision to make, the type that hangs over you until you do it. But I was petrified that I might miss my life, or get it wrong. The deeper I got into my career, the more trapped I felt.

I searched all corners of the world for the 'perfect thing' for me to do in order to play my part in leaving the world a little brighter with my presence. Spending many years waiting around for a perfectly plotted-out, single-minded plan to be miraculously revealed (in full) and land smack bang on my lap. And when I actually got pretty clear glimpses of what it could be, I longed for some external person to confirm that I had it right and to give me permission to get on with it.

I was *so* in my head... weighing up, pondering and questioning all the possible paths, petrified that I might choose the wrong one. I was stuck in inaction, waiting to be handed the map from the big G himself before I set off along my perfect path. I thought it was all about striving and doing, not being and embodying.

Through my own disillusion, time wasting, and working with loads of women who feel the same I have come to the conclusion that our Soul Purpose comes down to two things:

1. Be The Light

To 'be the light' you need to follow the things that light you up, so you can show up in life filled up and whole. You don't need a special job to 'be the light'; in fact you don't need any job at all. You can 'be the light' in the grocery store, you can 'be the light' while cooking dinner, you can 'be the light' on the world's most boring conference call, you can 'be the light' while updating your Facebook status, you can 'be the light' by being there for a friend or a stranger who needs a smile.

2. Be authentically you

There is no perfect path, only a perfectly authentic You – full of contradictions, uniqueness and gifts. It is your You-ness that allows you truly to light up the world with your presence. Your You-ness is lifetimes in the making. It is your flaws, your quirks, your weirdness, your ancestral history, your gifts, your humor, and your imperfections. Your light and message will come through you regardless of what path you choose. Your authentic self emerges when you follow what lights you up, or in other words, when you do what you love. And then do it in a way that only you can.

Our soul is always calling us towards what will light us up.

Our ego tries to trick us into thinking that it has to be more complicated. It cannot understand how it could be so simple as following what lights us up. But when we follow what we love over and over again, we stumble upon our calling without even realizing it. When we lose ourselves in the doing, we step out of the way and allow the light to flow through us.

And it feels freaking fantastic.

I've spent years trying to work out what my purpose is. Trying to fit it into a perfect little box with a step-by-step plan before I would even consider taking the leap. I looked at my strengths, listed my gifts, tried to work out the message my soul wanted to share, but still I held back because I couldn't see every single little step along the way. I wanted to know the final destination before I took the first step. All of the possibilities, purposes and callings would toss and turn in my head, but I was not acting on any one of them. I was waiting by the phone for the Universe to call saying, 'Hey guuuuurl, so this is your purpose.'

The amount of time I spent pondering whether I should be a writer, an actor, a life coach, a healer, an artist, a director, or a fashion designer is absolutely ridiculous. It doesn't matter if I write books, bake cakes, make movies, design cowboy boots, or tap dance on a piano.

It doesn't matter if I take photos, do speeches, run a country, teach kids, paint pictures, write comedy or host a TV show... As long as it lights me up, I will bring my own unique light to everything that I do. The only things that matters is doing the things that light you up over and over again and letting the light shine authentically through you.

Follow the trail of things that light you up and lose yourself in the doing. Before long you will find yourself right in the center of your purpose and the life you are called to live.

WORK YOUR LIGHT

Are you waiting for a perfect sign from the Universe
to tell you what your Soul Purpose is?

What can you lose yourself in because you love doing it so much?

PEOPLE CAME
FROM AFAR TO
BASK IN HER LIGHT.

△
YOU'VE BEEN WORKING ON
YOU FOR LIFETIMES

You're way more than the days that have breathed through you this life. You're also all of the lifetimes that came before. You're male and female, gay and straight, black and white, confident and shy, fat and thin, tall and small, a leader and a follower. And more. All of these experiences have polished your soul into the most magnificent expression that is your authentic self.

You = complete masterpiece.

Your soul has many facets. Imagine a fingerprint; your soul is a million times more intricate than that. If you put together all of the fingerprints of all of the people you have been, you would not even get close to fathoming how much of a unique masterpiece you are. You've been working on you for lifetimes.

It's why dogs seem to have a personality even when they are just small pups. The seeming personality is the light shining through their beautiful unique little soul. A part of them has experienced much more than the mere number of days since they were born.

You came in knowing. You came in with wisdom beyond your years, weeks, months, and days. This is the part of you that longs to be seen. This is the part of you that is ready right here and now to let the light shine through and emerge.

WORK YOUR LIGHT

Sitting comfortably, put your hand on your heart, and gently close your eyes. Breathe deeply and really sink into the space of your heart where your soul lives. Rest there awhile.

Imagine a multifaceted crystal in your heart center, slowly spinning. This is the eternal part of you, the fingerprint of your soul. As it spins around slowly, allow yourself to really absorb and embody all of the wisdom and all of the magnificent beauty that is You.

Ask your soul:

What wisdom do you have for me that can help right now?

What part longs to step forward right now?

What part is ready to emerge?

THE EGO TRUSTS THAT WE ARE SEPARATE AND GO THROUGH LIFE ALONE. **THE SOUL TRUSTS** THAT WE ARE ALL CONNECTED AND THUS NEVER REALLY ALONE. **THE UNIVERSE TRUSTS** THAT THE EGO WILL GET LONELY AND LISTEN TO THE SOUL.

△

THE EGO, THE SOUL, AND THE SPIRIT

We are divine beings having a human experience, here to grow, evolve and journey back to Source. Sometimes that human experience can be full of extreme joy and exhilaration. And sometimes being a spiritual being in a human body can be plain hard.

Getting to know the voices of our ego, soul, and spirit is extremely helpful when it comes to answering our highest callings.

The ego (our human self)

Our ego is the human part of us that sees itself as separate, as 'me' against 'them.' *A Course In Miracles* explains it 'like sunbeams thinking they are separate from the sun, or waves thinking they are separate from the ocean.' We are each sunbeams from the same sun and drops of water from the same ocean.

Often running off a program of fear, the ego is the inner critic, the judge, the victim, and the bully who thinks it is always right and has all the answers. Driven by a fear of 'everyone is out to get me' and 'there is not enough for everyone,' the ego sees the world as unfair and unsafe. It finds it hard to trust others, it lives in the past, it *loves* to create drama and feel sorry for itself (a lot). The ego tends to like things to be hard, believing that we need to 'work' to find our calling (if we are lucky enough to find it).

The ego is driven by a core fear, which colors the lens though which we see the world. When we are living in ego town, we are controlled by our fears. When we are living in a world of fear we are living in our shadow.

It's important to remember that we need our ego in order to survive on this planet. However, our life will flow more when our ego is serving and supporting the callings of our soul.

The soul (our ancient self)

The soul is the part of us that we carry from lifetime to lifetime. It is our ancient self. Both deep and hearty, it is a culmination of all the wisdom of the ages that you have trodden and the unique soul gifts that you have mastered over lifetimes.

Each life and experience adds to your authentic imprint. While it has wisdom through lessons learned, it can also carry trauma and patterns from past hurts. Lifetime after lifetime, we enhance our soul's growth, with the purpose of coming back home to our true essence (our divine self).

When a client comes to me in their dark night of the soul, I cannot help but celebrate. The extreme loss, heartbreak, or crumbling allows the ego to loosen its grip and admit it doesn't have all the answers, which leaves space for the light of the divine self (spirit) to come flooding in.

The spirit (our divine self)

The spirit is our divine connection to Source. It is the part of us that is connected to everything in the Universe. It is the spark in our eyes, the spring in our step, the sunshine on our face. It is the part of us that knows that we are whole and complete. It's grace. It's our higher self. It's God. It's pure light.

When our heart cracks open, a space is created for our soul to come through. When our soul cracks open, it allows the grace of spirit to come through. When our spirit, soul, and ego are working in harmony, the light of spirit (Source) is able to come flowing through our unique soul, body, and mind, and we are truly able to *work our light* in a way that only we can.

△

YOU ARE DIVINE

'Although you appear in earthly form, your essence is pure consciousness. You are the fearless guardian of divine light.'
RUMI

You are divine in every sense of the word: an expression of Source energy – light in human form. The ego leads us to believe we are separate from Source (and each other), and that we need to work to find our wholeness, love, and purpose. And if we are lucky enough to find it, we'd better cling onto it with all of our might for fear of losing it.

This denial of our divine nature leads us on endless searches outside of ourselves. We look to others to feel love. We look to something outside of ourselves to worship. We wait for people to give us permission to shine or feel whole and complete.

Whereas we already are all that we seek, we only have to turn our gaze in. Wholeness, happiness, and love are your birthright. As a baby there was no part of you that doubted your wholeness. As a result you lit up the world without even trying.

Love, light, wisdom, happiness, and wholeness are available to you 'on tap' at every moment because they are what you are at your core. And they're waiting for you to let them in.

MANTRA

I am connected to the never-ending flow of light. Everything I am searching for is ready to flow through me right now.

THE UNIVERSE IS
ALWAYS EXPANDING.
**YOU ARE PART
OF THE UNIVERSE.**
EXPANSION IS YOUR
NATURAL STATE.
IF YOU RESIST YOUR
EXPANSION, YOU
RESIST WHO YOU ARE.
**EXPAND INTO YOUR
BIGNESS NOW.**

△

ONENESS VS. ALONENESS

One of the most challenging things about being a spiritual being in a human body is the feeling of separation. Isolation.

Aloneness

While your soul is currently in a physical body (which is separate from others), you are part of a larger whole. A oneness beyond identity, body, and words. And somewhere deep down our soul remembers this. For souls who have experienced more than just the Earth plane, this Earth experience can feel horribly isolating. For our true essence knows that we are pure beings of light, love, and Oneness from Source having a human experience. You are divine.

While I have been blessed with a beautiful family and have always been surrounded by many friends, I have battled with this feeling of loneliness my whole life. It was like I had this distant memory that it wasn't meant to be like this. I had no idea that so many people felt the same.

From an early age I craved meaningfulness and couldn't stand conversations for the sake of it. You know the ones. Where people's mouths are moving but your heart is saying: *This whole thing is fake and a complete waste of both of our time, but let's keep talking because it's better than being alone.* I have felt more alone in some relationships than I have out of them.

This lingering feeling of aloneness has seen me hold on to relationships, friendships, and jobs longer than was in my best interest. It's also seen me gossip and stay at parties later than I wanted. And then there's the binge TV-watching and eating. It's as if I clung on to all these things, just so it could fill up the big gaping hole I felt deep within me. If only I had realized that this gaping hole was my invitation to go within.

During my own darkest hours, when I was truly alone and unreachable to those around me, I eventually discovered what I already knew intellectually. Sometimes we just need to clear out the space and let our aloneness take over to realize that we are never really alone. We are one. What we are seeking is actually what we already are. It's our denial of our own divine nature that makes us feel separate. It's our seeing ourselves as separate that makes us feel so alone.

There is a presence, which I call 'Grace' or 'Source', waiting for us behind the gates of aloneness. A presence so subtle yet palpable, that if we let ourselves feel it, it would bring us to tears. No words can do it justice, but once felt none are needed. A presence so supportive, loving, soothing, and familiar, that it feels like coming home. It feels like coming home because, when we feel it, we are actually tapping into the glorious Source energy, of which we are all a part. This presence of 'oneness' is available to us in every moment (and it's why I adore Sourcing so freaking much, see page 182).

Sometimes it takes everything to go wrong for us to give up the fight and give in to its warm embrace. Our soul knows the way. Listen to its whispers and follow the trail.

We are all bundles of divine cosmic Source energy buzzing around in human bodies. We see ourselves as separate, when really we are all going through the same thing. The same journey back home to oneness.

We are here to remember our divine nature and embody it in human form. We are not our body, our mind or our emotions. We are souls having an experience of body, emotion, and mind. The sooner we see ourselves as part of the greater whole and thus never really alone, the sooner we come home to the beautiful divine wonder that we naturally are (and the less alone we will feel).

We have chosen our bodies as perfect vehicles to express our divine light. Through these bodies, and the healing of our emotions, we express that light in our own way. The moment we try and be more like someone else, we get in the way and actually stop that effortless flow of light from streaming through.

You were not born to be like someone else. You were born to be like You. To remember that despite all of your experiences you are a Divine Being of Light, and to let that light flow through your unique soul, emotions, and body.

This is not about being perfect; the opposite is true.

It's about being real, true, transparent, and authentically You. Cracks, bumps, flaws, and all. When the light shines through our imperfections, that's when we are truly able to touch other people's hearts and souls.

MANTRA

I am a divine expression of light. I embrace
my flaws and shine anyway.

Th
ereis
nosepar
ationweare
onethereisno
separationweare
onethereisnoseparat
ionweareonethereisnose
parationweareonethereis
noseparationweareonetherei
snoseparationweareonethereisn
oseparationweareonethereisnosepa
rationweareonethereisnoseparation
weareonethereisnoseparationweareon
ethereisnoseparationweareonethereisnosep
arationweareonethereisnoseparationweareone

ALONE
OR
ALLONE?

△

WE CHOOSE OUR PARENTS

Before entering into this life, we chose our parents based on our own soul growth and the messages we're here to share. I chose my parents extremely well. But, like most people out there... I didn't always think so!

A non-traditional family where the roles were reversed, my mum, a fashion designer, was the primary breadwinner working long hours and traveling around the world a few times a year. My dad, a P.E. teacher at a local high school, would collect my brother and me from school, and also do all the domestic stuff like cooking dinner, ironing, and making sure we did our homework, because he had more time.

My parents taught me the importance of education; I can do anything I want to, if I put my mind to it; and how to work hard for the things I wanted.

When I experienced my first awakening aged 14, I wished that I had been born into a family that spoke of spiritual things around the dinner table. I was bursting to share my experiences and thought psychologist, philosopher, healer, or mind body spirit author parents would have been much better for me.

I first met Sheila Dickson after my mum suggested I babysit her children. Sheila had just moved in two doors down from my family home in Collaroy on Sydney's Northern Beaches. Eighteen years old, I bounced into Sheila's house and chatted with her and her four adorable children, swapping life stories and only pausing when we needed to take a breath.

Despite the huge age difference (she was 39 at the time) it was an instant connection and felt like coming home. Before we knew it, four hours had passed and the kids were asking if they could go to bed. As soon as I got home I called her on the phone and we spoke for a couple more hours before planning to meet the next day to do each other's tarot cards. We have been the best of friends ever since and consider each other family.

When I was 25, I visited Sheila and her family in Singapore, where she was living at the time, and she organized a past-life regression session for me. I had always been fascinated by the topic after reading books such as *Many Lives, Many Masters* by Brian Weiss and was excited to experience it for myself.

When I arrived, a lovely lady called Toni greeted me. She led me into a state of relaxation, and then regressed me from lifetime to lifetime. It was like traveling around the world, but without the jetlag.

I was then taken between lives to when I was getting ready for this life. *So cool!*

First, I was shown the experience of choosing my 'body' for this life, and presented with three different sets of potential parents, based on what I wanted to bring to the world and my soul growth.

The first were a lovely couple, Trevor and Julie from sunny Sydney (my parents). The mother was strong, kind, ambitious, and highly creative. The father was emotionally sensitive, big-hearted, easygoing, and ahead of his time in that he was able to be a rock and support his wife in an age when that was not the norm. I would be born the eldest child of two.

The second was a Russian woman, Olesya, who had migrated to America where she fell in love with an American businessman. Ancestrally her family line had endured a lot, so she would look to me to make the most of all of the opportunities I would be blessed with. An only child, I would be born male and go on to be an Olympic swimmer.

The third option was a Scottish couple. Andy and Sheila Dickson (my friend!). They were extremely young and I would be a surprise pregnancy. The early years would be tough, as they would have to adjust to being parents. An the child of an ex-pat family, I would live in many countries around the world. The mother would embark on a deep spiritual path paving the way for me, and encourage my spiritual work. I would be born the eldest child of five.

The concept of 'choosing your parents' had always resonated with me, but this experience took it to a whole other level. It helped me truly appreciate that I had made the right choice, and all of the gifts that my parents had given me.

When I told Sheila, she told me that her husband always referred to me as 'the fifth Dickson child.' And, one day, when the family was together, they played a game where they had to write down the name of their favorite person that felt most like family... And every single one of them said it was me.

There are things working on a different level that are impossible to see, but can be felt. For me, finding and answering my calling took a lot of courage, inner knowing and determination – which, considering my calling is to awaken Lightworkers to their authentic light and soul's calling, is a pretty good path to tread.

Regardless of whether you had a wonderful childhood or a terrible one, it was the perfect playground for your soul's growth.

WORK YOUR LIGHT

What things (good and bad) did your parents teach you?

Why do you think you chose them as parents?

How has this added to your soul's growth and path?

△

I'M TALKING TO THAT PART OF YOU

Today, I'm talking to that part of you who yearns for more.

The part of you who knows exactly what you want beyond all else.

To that part of you who effortlessly believes that anything
is possible, and that it's possible in an instant.

I'm talking to that part of you who longs to break right
on through that self-imposed ceiling your mind has
created out of fear, lack, should, and could.

To smash and shatter it into a billion little pieces.

I'm talking to that part of you who longs, who
dreams, who dances, who wishes.

To the part of you that cheers, that laughs, that leaps, that bounds.

To that part of you who truly wants the best for others because
it deeply knows that there is more than enough to go round.

I'm talking to that part of you who knows what you
want and the exact next step to take to get it.

To that part of you who knows you're not broken and isn't the
slightest bit interested in perpetuating the story that says it's so.

To that part of you who knows the way and longs
to guide the rest of you back home.

Today, that's the part of you I'm talking to.

And I'm asking it to step forward and lead the way.

△

YOUR INNER GURU KNOWS BEST

*'Come out of the masses. Stand alone like a lion
and live your life according to your own light.'*
OSHO

Your Inner Guru knows best. Better than even the most guru-like of teachers: the wise ones, the saints, the sages, and the swamis.

Sometimes it's just tricky to hear what is being said before your head comes in and doubts it all. To differentiate the crazy voice from the wholehearted, enlightened, centered voice of your soul. Then there's the times we wish it didn't know best, and so clutch outwards for another opinion to contradict our guidance and rest our fears, while secretly hoping it didn't know best in the first place. *Hello getting back with the ex, staying in a job we hate, or trusting someone we knew we shouldn't.*

Eventually we realize that our Inner Guru *DID* know best. Annoying but true. And if we had listened to that niggling little voice in the first place, we would have probably saved ourselves a heck of a lot of time/pain/ money/pride.

It's comforting to realize that you have everything you could possibly need inside you to get through any obstacle. It doesn't mean it's going to be easy, but the more you nurture and listen to your Inner Guru, the clearer and louder the whisper gets.

Carve out a non-negotiable time every day and listen to that little voice inside you. Part III, Living in the Light, is packed full of ideas to help you connect with it.

You have everything you need inside you right now because your Inner Guru knows best.

WORK YOUR LIGHT

Put your hand on your heart, take a couple of deep breaths, and ask your Inner Guru to shed some light on your current situation.

My Inner Guru is telling me to...

▲

INAUTHENTICITY NO LONGER STANDS A CHANCE

We are entering a time in history when we are moving from patriarchy to matriarchy: force to flow; masculine to masculine-and-feminine in balance. A time when inauthenticity no longer stands a chance. Gone are the days when we are rewarded for being good girls and boys, just because we stick things out, do our time, and live the life of a lemming.

Perhaps you've noticed it in your own life. Friendships that once felt like they'd last forever are drifting, relationships that you've been clinging to are hanging by a thread, it's becoming harder and harder to show up to that job every day without your heart in it, and perhaps it's getting impossible to put on that chirpy face and fake your way through the day. Or pretend to care about stuff that you don't.

Pretending takes effort. And effort leaves us depleted.

Life is throwing things at us to bring us back to the most authentic, fluid version of ourselves. Our foundations are being shaken, with only the parts of us rooted in authenticity able to survive. Relationships, jobs, friendships, things that we once took for granted are falling away.

It can be painful – change almost always is – especially when the change happens to impact the very foundations below us. The rug is being pulled and many of us have no choice but to find somewhere new to put down our roots. Somewhere the ground is fertile and the view is sweet.

The more we resist the ebbs and flows of change, the harder it gets. It's as if the tectonic plates of our lives will continue to shake until we loosen our grip, let go of the reins, and throw our hands up in the air and cry, 'I surrender.'

It's not until this moment that you can ask your soul to lead.

Amen.

WORK YOUR LIGHT

What is becoming harder and harder for you to hold on to?

What is the Universe trying to tell you?

YOUR **SOUL** KNOWS THE QUICKEST WAY **HOME**.

△

LOOSEN YOUR GRIP

'You can only lose what you cling to.'
BUDDHA

You're either in flow with the Universe or you're not. If you're clinging to anything, you're resisting the natural flow of who you are.

The things we cling to are the things we most need to let go. The boyfriend, the coffee, the job, the friendship, the vino, the overworking, the people pleasing... whatever external thing you cling to, in an effort to feel whole or like you're enough.

The things we cling to often cover up our most vulnerable space – the one that is desperately scary to leave empty. But by keeping that space covered with something that doesn't serve us we prevent ourselves from receiving the things that will. And we cast a shadow on our light.

We cling on tightly because deep down we know that unless we control, cling to, and hold on, we feel that relationship, job, or [*insert your thing here*] might not stay on its own accord.

But in loosening our grip, we open space for the light to come in, and heal the part of us that doesn't feel whole. As *A Course In Miracles* tells us:

'Whatever we leave empty, grace will fill.'

If we can find the courage to surrender, then that thing we once clung to will either stay on its own accord or be replaced by something that is beyond any of our wildest dreams.

Loosen your grip. Grace is coming. It might be uncomfortable at first, but I promise it will be worth it in the end.

WORK YOUR LIGHT

What am I clinging to for fear of nothing coming to take its place?

Δ

THE WORLD NEEDS YOU CRACKED OPEN

'There's a crack in everything. That's how the light gets in.'
LEONARD COHEN

Be open to being cracked open. Wide open.

It is the difficult times that help us grow in leaps and bounds, and in ways we could only dream possible.

But first, they have to crack us open. And sometimes it hurts like hell. It's nature's way. And, whether you let it happen or not, it is going to happen. So surrender to the process and let life do its *thang*. It'll be worth it. It's how the light gets in.

△

I PRAY THAT YOU HIT ROCK BOTTC

I pray that you hit rock bottom.

The most painful time of your life.

I pray that you feel alone. Isolated. Deserted.

And you discover that what you thought was rock bottom is
actually a ledge, so you come crashing down even further.

And as you land, you are cracked open into a million – no – a billion
pieces – and have no idea how to put them back together.

I pray that while you are down there in the depths, the
only person you have to keep you company is you.

I pray that you choose to gather up the pieces.

And with no idea how and in what order, then begin
putting them back together, one by one.

Just right.

I pray for foundations mightier than the Acropolis.

And an inner light that shines so bright it dazzles the
corneas of anyone who cannot handle your bright.

I pray for skin as comfortable as a 10-year-old
tracksuit on a Saturday night.

And an inner light so bright that you can always find your way home.

I pray for the triumph of your soul.

And the return of You.

△

YOUR SUFFERING HAPPENED FOR YOU, NOT TO YOU

As hard as it is, the things that almost break us apart are also the things that came to make us whole. To rejig things enough to get you back into alignment. To smash the pieces, which were stuck together in the first place. To shake your foundations so you build new ones that no situation or person could ever break.

So love your suffering and don't fight it. It's there to lead you back to your most authentic, biggest, brightest self.

Stand out of the way and let the Universe get to work.

WORK YOUR LIGHT

What have your greatest sufferings taught you about yourself?

△

YOU'VE BEEN TRAINING FOR THIS FOR LIFETIMES

If you don't feel ready, if you feel unprepared, I want you to know that:

> **This moment right here, you've been training for it for lifetimes.**

If you are faced with the unbearable and your heart feels like it might just rip in two, the thing I want you to know is:

> **This moment right here, you've been training for it for lifetimes.**

When your head is filled with 'Who am I to do this?' 'What happens if it doesn't work out?' and 'She's so much better than me,' the thing I want you to know is:

> **This moment right here, you've been training for it for lifetimes.**

You're more ready than you think and the sooner you act the sooner you will look back around and realize that:

> **This moment right here, you've been training for it for lifetimes.**

SHE LEFT THE OLD STORY BEHIND HER AND STEPPED INTO A NEW ONCE UPON A TIME.

△

DON'T LET IT DEFINE YOU

Don't let someone's unconscious acts define you. Chances are the healing journey spurred on by their actions will result in you being even more whole than before it happened in the first place. If it hurts like hell, take solace in knowing that any kind of cracking open is always a blessing in the end (sometimes it just takes time, if only you could see things from the view that we do).

We are all each other's mirrors, reflecting back the parts that are not whole. And, annoying as it may sound, the people who press your buttons the most are actually the ones who help you grow the most. They are a blessing. Or a curse. They can be the things that make you expand or contract. The choice is yours.

Soul mates are the people who spur on your growth like no other. Souls who agreed prior to this life to play a vital role in our expansion. When meeting a soul mate you may experience a sense of remembering or familiarity. Soul-mate relationships are not necessarily all sunshine and roses, in fact more often than not they can be extremely difficult, as sometimes, in order for us to grow, we need to experience pain.

Some are here for a moment, some for a chapter, and some for forever. Take the lesson and let go of the rest.

WORK YOUR LIGHT

What are your most difficult relationships?
Are you being called to let go of the relationship or hold on to it?
What have they taught you or are they trying to teach you?

HER INNER LIGHT ALWAYS CALLED HER **HOME**.

△

COME HOME TO YOURSELF

*'The ache for home lives in all of us, the safe place
where we can go as we are and not be questioned.'*
Maya Angelou

We spend our lives searching, only to discover it was inside us all along. I'm a perpetual traveler. A searcher. Always looking for ways to grow, learn, ponder, and understand. The undercurrent of all my days on this planet has been filled with searching for that feeling of truly being at home, without even really knowing what I was searching for. I moved continents, countries, cities, and houses. To this day I have lived in over 30 homes!

I've journeyed to six out of seven continents (*Antarctica, I'm coming*) and had two jobs where traveling around the globe was my sole responsibility.

My heart has been touched by exquisite souls from many cultures and my lungs filled up with the most breathtaking views.

My spirit has flown with adventure and my mouth has dropped open in awe.

Still, despite all of these remarkable experiences, I always felt as though something was missing, that I was unable quite perfectly to find that place or person who would bring me that feeling of home.

Until I realized that the place wasn't physical and, while enhanced and made warmer by other people, it wasn't actually about anyone else in the least. It has nothing to do with bricks and mortar, beaches, mountains, forests, or skyscrapers. Like all things that truly matter, what I was searching for was within. Home is wherever I'm with me.

If you've been spending your life searching for your true home, know that it has been inside you all along.

AFFIRMATION

I am home.

△

WHEN DID YOU STOP BEING YOU?

Babies aren't afraid to shine their light and it's the reason why we can't take our eyes off them. However, as life goes on, we experience things that eventually lead us to retract or alter the way we show ourselves to the world – usually based on a belief that something must be wrong with us. We lose contact with the authentic spirit within us, which has been carefully sculpted over lifetimes, and keep our authentic light under a bushel.

WORK YOUR LIGHT

Think back to your childhood... What experiences can you remember that caused you to believe that something was wrong with you, or your authentic self was not enough? How old were you? What happened?

How did it make you feel?

Ask that younger version of you what they need to hear to feel loved and supported.

△

YOU ARE ALREADY DOING IT

The person you are trying to let go of.
That heartbreak that feels too big to bear.
You're already doing it,
And you are closer than you think.

The sadness that weighs on your shoulders.
The heaviness that sits like an elephant on your chest.
Breath by breath, you are moving through it,
And you are closer than you think.

The person you are praying to forgive.
That grief you are desperate to release.
You're already doing it,
And you're closer than you think.

The person you admire.
The woman you long to become.
You are her and she is you,
And you are closer than you think.

The vision you are striving towards.
That dream that feels out of reach.
You're already doing it,
And you're closer than you think.

The end will be unrecognizable from the picture in your head,
But you'll know it when you get there by the way you feel in your skin.

△

FILL YOURSELF UP

You are no use to anyone, if you are running on empty.

I used to feel guilty and selfish for putting myself first, and following those things that nourished my spirit. One day I remember working at home and my housemate Dana found me watching *Private Practice* while eating my lunch. *Addison Montgomery, I love you.*

Even though I had been working incredibly long days to get my business off the ground, I still felt guilty that I'd been 'caught' doing something that filled me up instead of working hard.

I didn't realize how much more I was able to give to others by filling up myself first. That little fact changed everything.

I've always known that fresh flowers light me up more than most things on the planet. But I spent many years waiting for someone else to buy them for me (how stupid was that). I got a bunch here and there, but on the whole the flowers didn't come.

Then I made a decision to give myself a weekly budget to buy the most gorgeous flowers I could find. So every Saturday I would take myself to the florist and pick my bunch. It felt fabulously extravagant.

At first I only let myself choose those that were good value. But then I stretched myself and bought the ones that lit me up the most. Before long, I had embarked on a deep love affair with the peony. Those flowers healed my heart more than anything else. The way they courageously open is breathtaking. And just when you think they can't open any further, they go and open some more.

Since making that simple decision to give my heart what it needs – beauty – my house has always been filled with the most beautiful flowers. It's a weekly ritual and worth every cent because when I look at them, my heart opens, my face softens, and light comes flooding in.

And the most fabulous thing is that once I started giving myself flowers I started receiving them too! The other day my fiancé, Craig, even surprised me with a subscription to Petalon, where they hand deliver a bunch of flowers, chosen especially for me, to my door every Wednesday!

Right now, as I sit writing this, I have a smile spread across my face because I'm sitting in the Queen's Rose Garden in Regent's Park in London surrounded by a kaleidoscope of thousands of beautiful roses inspiring me as I type. I am filled up and so my light effortlessly spills onto the pages.

The moment we stop nurturing and filling ourselves up, things just don't flow quite the same.

What nourishes you will be different from the next person. For my friend Amy Firth, it's knitting, Skyping her family, and playing music. For my Mum, it's walking along the beach, making things beautiful, and gardening. For my friend Jaqui Kolek, it's reading trashy magazines, getting a mani-pedi, and Vegemite on toast. The more you fill yourself up, the more you have to share with others

WORK YOUR LIGHT

Write a list of all the things that fill you up.

Pick one thing off the list that you can commit to giving yourself today.

△

WE ALL JUST WANT TO BE SEEN

We all just want to be seen, like really seen. Not glanced over and noticed, but for someone to take a moment and really witness the authentic light that flickers just beneath the surface. But we go about our lives, bumping into each other and not taking the time to stop and look.

The most intimate experience of my life was with a 50-year-old Croatian woman I had known for 5 minutes. I didn't even know her name. We met during a workshop led by Juilliard voice coach, Claude Stein. We were mostly a room full of strangers, and he instructed us to turn to the person next to us and look deeply into their eyes. *Like REALLY look into their eyes.* And witness the gorgeous soul standing directly in front of us. And at the same time, let that person truly see us. The real us. The deeper us. The us that we hadn't shown anyone before.

Before long, and without exchanging a word, my gorgeous partner and I began to sob. Deeply. It was unlike any other experience of my life. Precious. Sacred. A gift. It felt as though I was being truly seen for the first time in my life. I was humbled and overwhelmed by the beauty of the person before me, who until that point I hadn't even paused to notice. We carried on like this for 10 minutes. It was one of the best 10 minutes of my life.

After the exercise was over we hugged and looked around the room and there wasn't a dry eye in the house. I found out her name was Sanja, and she is now a true friend and part of my mastermind group.

This experience has been etched on my heart ever since, and made me understand that every human on the planet – no matter how soft or how hard, how open, or closed – just wants to be seen. *Like really seen.*

The greatest gift we can give another person is to witness truly their being here.

To see deeply and acknowledge the sacred soul that dwells within them and is longing to emerge.

After this, I came to realize how pretty much every problematic relationship I'd ever experienced was a result of either not being seen accurately or not seeing the other person accurately.

It brought to light how much of my life I'd spent holding back my biggest, truest, most authentic self, while secretly hoping someone else might see it. Spot it. Name it and call it forward. I'd spent so long keeping my light dimmed, while deep down hoping that someone would acknowledge all of the immense beauty that bubbled just below the surface. It dawned on me that I had spent too many years waiting for acknowledgment and permission for my brightest, most exuberant self to emerge.

That day marked the beginning of my conscious journey towards seeing the authentic light in other people and shining my own a little more brightly.

You have an authentic inner light, which has always been there and will never go away. An inner fire that no matter how dark it gets will continue flickering.

People can see it just by looking at you. It's that 'something special' that they see. It's that 'spark,' that 'twinkle' in your eyes.

Your light is your authentic self and you were born to shine it. You can't hide a light.

WORK YOUR LIGHT

Your presence is a gift. Rather than going through the motions, be truly present and let someone truly witness you today.

YOU CAN'T
HIDE **A LIGHT.**

△

SEE THE LIGHT IN OTHERS

'See the light in others, and treat them as if it's all you see.'
WAYNE DYER

One of the greatest offerings we can give another person is to witness truly their gifts. When we witness the gifts of another, we are actually witnessing the soul and light in them.

Such a simple and effortless act can have a life-changing impact. When we acknowledge the gifts of another, we raise them up and encourage them to shine a little bit brighter. This act not only feels wonderful, but it is impossible to do and not light up too.

WORK YOUR LIGHT

Light up someone's day today by truly witnessing them and acknowledging one of their gifts.

△

THE FEAR OF BEING SEEN

We have experiences, often stemming from childhood, where we decided that our authentic self was not enough. A significant moment when we decided that it was safer/easier/less painful to shine a little less. We decided to dim to fit in.

We don't need to have a conscious memory of these experiences for them still to affect us today. Our soul carries imprints from lifetime to lifetime, which hold wisdom gained from lessons learned, as well as past traumas that are waiting to be healed.

We are here to heal those traumas that are standing in our way and preventing us from stepping into our most authentic selves. When we step into our authentic power, we are unafraid of letting our biggest authentic self be seen, regardless of who is in front of us.

WORK YOUR LIGHT

Think back to a point in your life when you consciously decided that who you were wasn't enough. What happened? What does this younger version of you need to hear now?

△

DON'T DIM TO FIT IN

Don't dim your light to accommodate someone else's smallness. We are all born to shine big and bright. The Universe is expanding and you are part of the Universe, so expanding is part of your nature.

If someone makes you want to retract, notice, and slowly back away, they are not for you and you are not for them. Or better yet, find it within yourself to expand and shine your light anyway.

Flowers don't open and close according to who is walking by. They open and show their beauty regardless.

Light up no matter who is around you. When you do, you make it easier for your people to find you. And if others don't want to be around you, or you make them feel uncomfortable, it's because you are shining light on the fact that they are dimming to fit in themselves. And by you choosing to shine bright you may just inspire them to turn on their light too. Or not. Keep your light on anyway, and watch as life shines right back at you.

△

PEOPLE WHO CAN'T HANDLE YOUR BRIGHT

If you have kept your bigness restrained and your light dimmed, chances are the people in your life have gotten used to that.

All relationships are essentially an energetic agreement. Some are built around one person shining, others around two people shining at the same level, and others around two people happy for the other freely to shine bright (*the best kind*).

The moment one person decides to start rising up and allowing their light to shine, it changes the energetic agreement and can create some waves. That's completely normal.

Choose to shine anyway.

The relationships that are meant to last will adapt to the change in energy. Others won't. But that's because they were likely born under the proviso of 'I love you as long as you don't shine more brightly than me.' That's OK, not all people are meant to be in your life forever. But the lessons they teach us can still live on.

WORK YOUR LIGHT

Who in your life raises you up, wants you to win
and is genuinely happy when you shine?

Who in your life can't hack it if you shine more brightly than them?

△

MIRRORS

In order for other people to acknowledge us, first we need to acknowledge ourselves. The people in our lives are merely mirrors reflecting back to us what we believe about the Universe and ourselves. Mirrors reflecting back to us our shadow and our light.

If you are not feeling supported, maybe you are not supporting yourself. If people are not recognizing the beauty in you, it's likely to be because you are not recognizing the beauty in yourself. If people are not acknowledging your musical talents, perhaps you are not acknowledging them yourself. If people are not giving you the time of day, it's because you are not giving it to yourself.

WORK YOUR LIGHT

Look in the mirror and really see yourself as if seeing yourself for the first time. Look deeply into your eyes and ask yourself:

What am I not seeing in myself that longs to be seen?

△

YOU ARE THE HEROINE OF YOUR LIFE

You are the heroine of your life. If not you, then who? We are each writing our own story with us as the lead character.

The moment we realize that we write our own story is the moment we realize that we have control to do a rewrite. And unlike most movies, with you, the sequel is likely to be even better than the first.

In the depths of moving out of the apartment I had shared with my ex, I played back-to-back movies on my laptop while I packed up the house. I was feeling very sorry for myself, and when my friend Sheila called I burst into tears. She asked what had brought it on.

I thought back and said, 'Well, I've been watching an awful lot of Meryl Streep and Susan Sarandon films, which I adore, but they are always quite emotional.'

We then dug deeper and deeper to realize that all of my favorite films have a strong independent female lead that gives and gives but still ends up alone: *Stepmom, Thelma and Louise, Sophie's Choice, It's Complicated...* BINGO! My favorite kind of film was how I was living my life. As hard as it was, I banned myself from watching strong female lead dramas and decided to write a new story for myself.

WORK YOUR LIGHT

Take note which films you choose to consume and what archetype the hero or heroine embodies, then ask:

What kind of movie am I currently starring in? Is it

a drama or an adventure? A musical or a comedy?
A saga or a life-affirming inspirational?

What kind of movie do I want to be starring in?

What qualities does the main character
of that movie need to possess?

Δ

WHO AM I?

'Beauty begins the moment you decide to be yourself.'
Coco Chanel

I'm a massive Oprah fan. When I first moved to London I lived with my friend Jaqui from university. We would spend our hangovers (*of which there were many*) watching Oprah's 25th Anniversary box set on repeat. We'd joke, 'Do you reckon Oprah and Gayle get hungover and question themselves like us?'

Jaqui would roll down the stairs in her favorite hangover T-shirt with 'Who am I?' splashed across the front. And that pretty much summed up how I felt during those years.

Back to the box set... The most moving moment for me was when Oprah told the story of a woman saying to her, 'Watching you be you makes me want to be more me.'

Those words continued to sit in my heart. Like many people in their twenties, I attached who I was to what I did, the roles I played, and the things I had learned to be good at, rather than following what lit me up (e.g. the hard worker, the ambitious creative, the daughter, the friend, the supportive girlfriend). But that wasn't who I really was... I could feel so much more inside of me that was bursting to come out.

Looking back I can join the dots and survey the signs of my life. But in those days (*especially the hungover ones*) I felt alone and lost. I was so attached to what other people thought that I didn't let my real self emerge.

The only thing missing was me.

PRAYER

Divine Mother, thank you for helping me remember
the truth of who I am, especially when it is different
from the truth of who I thought I was.

△

WHO ARE YOU?

Our instant response to this question is usually to list off name, age, sex, occupation, where we were born, where we live, relationship status, blah, blah, blah...

But that's not who we are. Not really. So we dig a little deeper and describe who we are based on our personality and things that the world has said about us: I'm a hard worker, I'm a good friend, I'm ambitious, I'm social, I'm creative, I'm a good cook....

But that's not who we are, or who we really came here to be. There's so much more to us than that. Secret parts that long to be expressed beyond the box that we have been put into or keep ourselves inside.

When we peel back the layers over and over again, we are able to find the wisdom and truth of our being, the essence that we are here to share. This is your magic, your gift to the world.

The part of you that is timeless and knows exactly what lights it up. The part of you that is expansive and waiting for you to remember, to discover, to unlock, and set it free.

WORK YOUR LIGHT

Standing in front of a mirror, look deeply into your eyes and ask the part of you that knows, 'Who am I?'

Allow it to answer. What you receive doesn't have to make sense as the purpose here is to peel back the layers and let your deeper self emerge. Keep repeating this question and response over and over again.

You may start by saying, 'I am a mother,' 'I am a daughter,' 'I am a hard worker,' 'I am a nurturer,' 'I am a fantastic listener,' 'I am wise,' 'I am love,' 'I am a tribal leader,' 'I am a mystic,' 'I am ready to rise up,' 'I am grace.'

Be open to being surprised. Peel back the layers and let your deepest self emerge.

△

ASK THE PART OF YOU THAT KNOWS

There's a part of you that knows the answer to everything you seek: your path, your purpose, which direction to move in, and exactly when to leap.

Before you incarnated, it received a mandate from spirit and, upon hearing this request, this part of you jumped right on in and couldn't wait to begin.

Willing to be ignored time and time again, the part of you that knows vowed never to give up, no matter how long it takes.

The part of you who knows, knows that you are in exactly the right place to do everything that you set out to do.

For the part of you who knows also knows that deep down you know too.

You're ready.

You know the next step.

The part of you who knows is calling you right now and wanting you to get ready to leap.

△

LEAP INTO YOURSELF

*'Don't dance around the perimeter of
the person you want to be.'*

GABRIELLE BERNSTEIN

Leap.

Take the plunge.

Don't waver.

Dive right in.

Into your wholeness.

Your You-ness.

Contradictions, imperfections, oddness, fabulousness, and all.

In doing so, sure you may find that you don't quite fit in, but that's just because in stepping into your bigness you might just need a little more room.

WORK YOUR LIGHT

How can you leap more into yourself?

THINK WITH YOUR SOUL.

△

FACE THE NIGGLE

That niggling feeling.

That annoying, niggling feeling.

That inconvenient, annoying, niggling feeling.

Try as you might, it's there. And it ain't going anywhere.

I spent years ignoring niggling feelings. Throwing my best dollops of stubbornness, ego, post-rationalization, and numbing-out at them. It's exhausting. And until you face it, life just throws you more bait to awaken the niggle. To draw your attention to the light within you that is bursting to come out.

Face the niggle now.

The niggle is your soul tugging at your sleeve, doing its best to get your attention before it has to turn up the heat. Listen now, if you don't face the niggle, the Universe will throw something in your path. And then you will regret that you didn't answer the niggle in the first place – *LOL*.

WORK YOUR LIGHT

What is your niggling feeling trying to tell you?

Who are you here to be?

FOLLOW YOUR INTUITION – ESPECIALLY WHEN IT DOESN'T MAKE SENSE.

△

ANSWER THE ACHE

We each have within us an aching that is craving to be met. It's not a physical ache and it isn't a mental one. It's much deeper than either of those.

We came into this life with it and, if it's not tended to, it will be right there when we die. It drives our deepest desires (our best decisions and our worst). It's lying beside us when we wake up in the night and while we make a cup of tea. It's there through the highs and all of the lows. The ache is your soul calling, and no matter what you do to ignore it, numb it out, or die it down, it will never go away.

Until we take the time to invite it to sit down and share with us, we will always feel a little uncomfortable. A touch off-kilter. Like something isn't quite right. Answer the ache.

WORK YOUR LIGHT

What is your soul aching for?

What is your soul trying to tell you?

What small thing can you do to answer that ache today?

△

YOU ARE NOT GOING TO MISS YOUR LIFE

The only way to miss your life is to spend it thinking that you are going to miss it. There is no right way, perfect answer, or correct road to take.

Work it out as you go and then you just dance extra quick.

It's just as important to get it wrong, as it is to get it right. In fact, getting it wrong is often a prerequisite for getting it right. Your stuff-ups, your fails, your confusion, your despair. All of these things make up *your* path less trodden.

Be OK with putting your hands up in the air and saying, 'I have no freaking idea where this is all leading.'

Take a deep, deep breath and walk ahead anyway.

WORK YOUR LIGHT

If you weren't afraid, what would you do?

△

MY SOUL IS CALLING ME TO...

Part III

WORK
YOUR
LIGHT

Answering your soul's callings

IF NOT YOU, WHO? IF NOT NOW, WHEN?

EMMA WATSON

△

YOUR SOUL IS ALWAYS CALLING

You're never too old to answer your calling and it can never be too late. For the truth of the matter is that your soul is always calling, it was calling yesterday, it is calling today, and it will be calling next week.

Answering the calling of your soul isn't a one-time act; it's a perpetual conversation. It's not actually about doing one big thing, or finding one single answer to the great big question: 'What is my purpose?' It's doing hundreds and thousands of little things in that direction, one after the other. It's through following each and every little call – a step here and a leap there – that we find ourselves living the life we are called to live.

Once we find this higher calling it seems like it 'just happened,' but in reality it has been in the process of happening for ages. Your soul knows your path.

Keep listening to, and acting on, the whispers each and every day and before you know it you'll be well on your way.

Your soul is always gently pointing you in the right direction, and subtly edging you closer towards the things that light you up. If you wait to find out exactly where your path is heading before you act, you will never experience the bliss of walking your path.

WHAT IS YOUR SOUL CALLING YOU TO **DO RIGHT NOW?**

△

IT'S HARDER TO IGNORE A CALL THAN TO ANSWER IT

If this book has made its way into your hands, it's probably because your soul spoke and you responded. It doesn't matter if you bought it yourself, it fell off the shelf, or someone gave it to you.

The soul speaks in feelings, in longings, in yearnings, in deep knowing, in vibration, in signs, in nature, in people. It centers itself in the heart, and carries within it a blueprint for your life. You can't hear the calling of your soul if you don't create space in your day to listen to it.

The best way I've found to connect with the voice of the soul is regular meditation. I'm not talking just walking or doing something that is meditative, but rather sitting down and truly listening – every single day. Your soul has secrets to share, but you need to carve out the time and space to hear them before you can act on them.

Once the voice of the soul has been heard, it cannot be unheard. Try as you might, if you ignore the calling of your soul, life becomes uncomfortable. You may find that you try to soothe that aching feeling by things in the external world. This may work for a little while, but eventually that niggling feeling comes back, and each time it does, it needs more to turn it down.

Don't waste your effort trying to ignore the call; create the space in your life to hear the daily whispers. The more you listen the louder the calling will get.

WORK YOUR LIGHT

Are you carving out time every day to listen
to the callings of your soul?

Download the Light Sourcing meditation
at www.lightisthenewblack.com

△

SOUL CALLINGS VS. THE CALLINGS OF YOUR SOUL

*There is no greater gift you can receive than
to honor your calling. It's why you were born.
And how you become most truly alive.*

OPRAH WINFREY

Your soul is eternally calling you in the direction of your highest path. Answering your soul's calling is not about a single revelation; rather it is a lifelong dance.

Your soul knows the way and so is always calling you in the direction of your highest path. But in order for your highest calling to be revealed you first need to act on all of the little calls along the way. It's impossible to find the bigger calling without first answering the daily callings of your soul.

Have you been holding off answering the whispers of your soul because you are trying to work out your highest calling first? (In other words, wanting to know the end destination before taking the first steps?)

WORK YOUR LIGHT

What is one small practical thing that you can do in the
next 24 hours to answer the callings of your soul?

△

YOU WERE BORN KNOWING

I want to tell you right now that whatever you are called to do, that is your calling. Following whatever lights you up is how you will light up the world. How you will most light up the world is your calling.

The world needs you lit up.

Deep down, you already know what you long for. What your soul yearns for. What you came here to do. There is nothing for you to discover, rather more of You to uncover.

To remember. To recall. To call back home.

You are in exactly the right place to answer your calling now. You don't need to know the whole plan. You don't even need to know where it is leading. You just need to take the next step.

In my Soul Readings, I have found that deep down everyone knows what they came here for. Deep down they know exactly what they long to do. Deep down, their calling is actually clearer than they could ever imagine. But the things that trip most people up are:

- Wanting to label what it is, rather than just following what lights them up.

- Looking for some kind of approval that the thing that lights them up is actually the right thing, and that they are good enough for it.

- Feeling like they have a plan of exactly how it is going to work out before they consider leaping towards it.

YOUR SOUL HAS
ALL THE **ANSWERS**.
THE ONLY WAY
TO HEAR THEM IS
TO **GO WITHIN**.

△

CAREER VS. CALLING

'You can lose your job but you can't lose your calling.'
MARIANNE WILLIAMSON

A job is something that you show up to every day to get paid for. Whether or not you enjoy it, a job is seen as 'work.'

A calling is something that you do because you love it and can't imagine doing anything else. It's something that you would do for free for the joy of it and sometimes it feels like this is the exact reason you were put on Earth.

A job forces you to fit into a mold. A calling expands with you.

Your calling doesn't have to be big and lofty, and it doesn't have to be your job. It might be being a supportive mother or a peace activist for the UN.

▽

My whole life I knew I wanted to touch people's hearts through my creations. I didn't know how I was going to do it, but I knew I couldn't ignore that yearning deep in my soul. My work was always my number-one priority and I chose a hardworking mother to ingrain this into me further.

Torn between spirituality, healing, writing, creativity, and business, I went to art school and then took a degree in communications, while spending my free time and money learning as much as I could about soul growth, metaphysics, life purpose, intuition, and consciousness.

I pursued a career in advertising because I knew I wanted my ideas to reach a mass audience. But, to be completely honest, I chose it because I thought it was the most socially accepted way for me to shine my light. I was an undercover Lightworker. I convinced myself that advertising would allow me to put my energy out there, and one day, when I had 'made it,' I would be able to really change things.

Naturally ambitious, I worked day and night on ideas to impress creative directors and get my first job. The day I got the phone call offering me the position of junior creative, I was over the moon. Thinking up ideas all day long, understanding the way people think, working with famous directors, going on shoots, and being taken out to lunch... There was so much about this job that I loved, but at the end of the day that niggling feeling was waiting for me, whispering that this job was not my highest path.

Six months into the job, the company merged with another global agency and I was made redundant. Without enough perspective or experience to realize that it wasn't personal, I felt completely devastated and ashamed. My inner voice was screaming that this was my out to follow my true calling, but my ego saw leaving as an act of defeat. A month later, I found a job at another ad agency.

About five years later, having moved to London and broken into the industry there, I was exhausted and depleted. I enjoyed so much of my job, but it was energetically draining. Endeavoring to fill the space inside, I turned to coffee, food, and social drinking to keep me going. The creative department ran on fear and everyone was constantly looking over their shoulders, worried that at any moment they'd lose their job if their last ideas were not good enough. While I knew I was good at my job, I also knew there was so much more of me that was not being used. Each night I'd arrive home completely exhausted, but still feeling like there was something in my heart that had not been expressed in my job.

When I heard Marianne Williamson say, 'You can lose your job but you can't lose your calling,' I realized that instead of forging my own path, I had been trying to fit into a job-shaped box. My job was on loan to me, but my calling was something that no one could ever take away.

I looked around but couldn't see any job that fitted the mold of what I was called to do. Knowing that whatever we leave empty God will fill, I quit my job and prayed. I updated my website so it boldly stated who I was and my unique and eclectic mix of passions and gifts. These included ambitious, big-hearted, creative, on a mission to change the world through my creations, big thinking, authentic writer, lover of travel (Romany spirit), excitable, hardworking, down to earth, believer, soulful. I affirmed over and over again:

My creations uplift and inspire people all around the world. I serve the world by being me.

I kid you not, the very next week I was head-hunted for the most amazing job ever – paid to travel the world making the gray spaces brighter – with the Let's Color Project.

I had leapt and the Universe caught me. A couple of weeks later I headed off on a world trip with an amazing team of big-hearted creatives filming, photographing, and documenting the journey. We brought color to orphanages, schools, community squares, and streets. I was getting paid amazing money (double my previous salary) to use my creativity, huge heart, and adventurous spirit to make the world a more colorful place.

I had listened to the callings of my soul and I felt more alive than ever.

WORK YOUR LIGHT

Do you currently have a job or a calling?

Do you have something more in you that
longs to be shared with the world?

△

YOUR TREASURE CHEST OF ᴄ

You have more gifts than you could imagine. Thousands of them, all at your fingertips. Just waiting to be unwrapped. The things that come naturally to you, the things you might not even notice because they are so innate, so inbuilt, so effortless, and so abundant. And then there are the gifts that somewhere along the way you began to doubt. The ones you chose to put in the closet, thinking that you might not be enough. You are. More than enough.

Just because you are not using your gifts right now doesn't mean they aren't there: the musician, the comic, the poet, and the dancer, the listener, the optimist, the cook, and the nurturer. The more you remember and claim these parts of you, the more effortlessly your authentic self will emerge. Your authentic self is bountiful, it's magic.

They are the things that you love doing, many of which you probably already do for free. The things that people thank and compliment you for doing. The thing you can lose hours doing because it consumes you. And just because you're happy to do them for free, doesn't mean you have to. You deserve to be rewarded for doing what brings you joy. In fact, it's increasingly becoming the most abundant way forward.

In order to light up the world, we first need to acknowledge how much of a unique gift we are to it. It doesn't matter who you are, you have more gifts than there are minutes in the day. It is the wonderful mishmash of these gifts that makes you, YOU.

This may seem overwhelming and a bit uncomfortable, but it is true. As you recognize your gifts people around you begin to notice them too, and all of a sudden you start attracting opportunities, which bring these gifts to life.

Don't squeeze your amazingness into a square box. Take all the space you need and spill over the sides.

I'd been living in London for about six months, holding out for a job at one of the top ad agencies. I'd seen creative director after creative director and they all said the same thing, 'We love your work but we don't know where to put you.' The ad industry in Australia was quite different from London. As well as having TV, film, and print experience, I had also done online films and websites. What should have been my point of difference was actually working against me, and suddenly I realized that I had been trying to fit into a London-shaped box.

I was almost out of money, but refused to take a job that wasn't my dream job, and was too proud to go home. Then, when I thought about the people that I admired most, I discovered that they didn't try to fit in to succeed, they embraced their uniqueness and forged their own path. So I wrote down all the things that were unique about me and created an affirmation, which encapsulated it all: 'I have a job that only I can do and I am rewarded beyond my wildest dreams. My creative ideas spread all over the world.'

One month later, a creative director called me out of the blue. I hadn't worked with him directly, but I'd met him over a glass of bubbly while celebrating a new business win for the ad agency. We got talking and I told him about my love for travel and he made some Australian jokes and taught me what a Scotch egg was.

He explained that the job was unique, but he thought I would be perfect for it. Hearing those words, I gave myself a high five knowing that my affirmation had called this one in!

I was to travel around the world nonstop for Skype and share my journey through writing, photography, film, and social media: five continents in 33 days, meeting amazing people, and visiting 27 cities (*pretty much all of which were on my vision board*). The only catch was that I had to do all of this while in perpetual motion (including sleeping). Extremely challenging, it was also one of the most amazing experiences of my life.

In recognizing my own gifts, and choosing not to fit into a normal-shaped box, I had attracted a job that was not only perfect for me, but also I was perfect for it. I was out of my comfort zone a lot of the time, but as a result I realized I had more gifts that I hadn't even known were there.

The old way of put your head down and just fit in is coming to an end. When we truly embrace our gifts in an unapologetic way we create a special kind of magic that is impossible to mimic. As we acknowledge our gifts, the world acknowledges them too. In the Age of Light we will all be rewarded and supported for doing what comes naturally to us, for sharing our unique gifts.

You don't necessarily need to go out and quit your job to express your gifts. When you own your gifts, your life will expand with you. Don't fit into a box that already exists. Discover more, overspill and share them all now.

MANTRA

I have a job that only I can do and I am
rewarded beyond my wildest dreams.

△

THE NEVER-ENDING GIFT LIST

Name your gifts. There are no wrong answers. It could be anything from being a good listener, to having a great sense of humor. It could be the fact that you don't beat around the bush and have a special knack for saying what you mean. It could be that you have a huge heart or are an animal lover. It could be the fact that you have beautiful handwriting or that you feel what other people are feeling. It doesn't matter what your gifts are, just that you keep uncovering them. The more you name, the more will emerge.

WORK YOUR LIGHT

Write a list of 10 of your unique and eclectic mix of gifts now. Keep this list going and add to it as you uncover more and more every day.

1.

2.

3.

4.

5.

6.

7.

8.

9.

10.

△

YOU DON'T HAVE TO STICK AT IT

You don't have to stick at it just because you have been sticking at it for so long. The longer you stick at something the harder it can be to let go. But no matter how long you have been clinging, holding together, slogging away, it's still going to be easier to let go today than it will be tomorrow.

You can do this.

While you might feel like the years and the struggles and all the effort will have been for nothing, I promise you the opposite is true. You will not be left with nothing and nothing is ever wasted. That inner voice that is calling you, she has no plans to let up. Drown her out all you like, but there she'll be sitting on your chest the moment you wake up.

She wants the best for you.

Listen to her whispers, her gnawing and her cries. She can see the vista coming up ahead, and there's a reason she won't give you a reprieve. The only way to stop her nagging, her kicking, and her screaming is to loosen your grip.

Trust, surrender, let go, give in.

The lead-up to surrendering might take an awful long time. But once the act is done, what is meant for you will come to you immediately. And then you'll wonder why you didn't act sooner in the first place.

WORK YOUR LIGHT

What are you sticking at just because
you've been sticking at it so long?

△

A PRAYER FOR LETTING GO

Divine Mother,

May my soul be stubborn and my spirit fierce.

May I find the strength to let go when I have
nothing lined up to take its place.

May I find the courage to listen, especially
when I don't like what I hear.

And when I pretend I can't hear you, please
speak up louder than before...

For that is when I need you most.

Thank you. And so it is.

△

SHADOW CALLINGS

Everyone has a calling but not everyone has the courage to answer it. In fact, most people ignore their calling completely. The fact that you are reading this book is a pretty awesome feat.

Drawing inspiration from Julia Cameron's concept of the shadow artist, a 'shadow calling' is when we don't have the courage to answer our highest calling and so settle for something halfway. It's the managers who long to sing, the film producers who want to direct, the agents who were meant for the stage, the project managers who yearn to make art, the historians who are called to make history, and the copywriters who have 10 books in them.

**Only you know if you are in a
shadow career for your soul.**

Watching from the sidelines is agony. Your gifts are there to be expressed, and if you don't actively do something with them, the Universe will find a way to coax them out of you. But it might be in a way that doesn't serve you.

Deep down I always knew that I wanted to write, create, heal, and uplift. I found myself in my shadow calling working as a copywriter in advertising. There was a lot that I loved about that job because I was getting paid to write and create. But, at the end of each day, I felt dissatisfied because I was not consciously expressing my gifts as a healer and uplifter.

And so life demanded me to be the healer and the uplifter, regardless of my career. My boyfriend had chronic depression and so I was spending a lot of my energy looking at ways to get him through that. Several of my close friends were also suffering from depression.

At the time I was working in a creative team with a guy who was a quadriplegic. I chose to work with him because he inspired me so much. Unable to move from the neck down, his glasses had a laser chip in them that was connected to his computer and he would art direct in Photoshop by moving his head. We shared an office and had nurses in every hour to give him water, feed him, change his position, and take him to the bathroom. If they weren't available I would step in. While we were working together he had to have an emergency tracheotomy, which meant that he needed help clearing his chest every hour or so. Pretty much all parts of my life demanded that I be the uplifter. But I was running on empty, so it was exhausting.

Now I see that all of this was the Universe trying to wake me up to my path and this period of my life was a blessing.

The longer you stay in a situation that doesn't fit, the harder it is to take a leap towards your highest calling. I know it's difficult when you've worked so hard at something and how letting all of that go is a scary prospect. But in the end, it won't be as scary and hard as you think. Nothing is ever wasted. The sooner you leap, the sooner you will look back at this moment and say, 'I'm *so* glad that I found the courage to leap.'

WORK YOUR LIGHT

Are you in a shadow calling or your true calling?
What is your soul calling you to do?

△

SHAKE IT OFF

It's easy to get stuck in the trap of doing something just because you're good at it. Or just because you've spent a lot of time being good at it and are afraid of letting it go.

The more capable you are at doing things, the harder it is to differentiate your natural gifts from the ones that you've learned or forced yourself to be good at – especially if your motivation is approval.

WORK YOUR LIGHT

What have you learned to be good at that you don't enjoy?

△

MULTIPLE CALLINGS

'Where would you have me go?
What would you have me do?
What would you have me say, and to whom?'
A Course in Miracles

We need more conscious people in power in all pockets of society. Perhaps you were called to work in one particular industry and then another. Don't be hard on yourself if you find that overnight you feel called to do something else. Nothing is ever wasted. Remember, your soul is always calling, every single moment of the day; it's not a one-time deal.

When we devote our lives to being of service, we will always be led. It doesn't mean that you had it wrong before. All that matters is that you listen, trust, and act on the call today. When you do that, all that has been held back will be delivered to you and you will be supported every step of the way.

WORK YOUR LIGHT

What do you feel called to do right now?

△

THE DOTS JOIN IN THE END

It wasn't till two weeks ago that the dots finally joined for me about being a writer. I was in Paris with my parents, who were visiting from Australia. Knowing that I was going to be writing this book, my mum brought over a children's book I wrote when I was 13 for a school assignment.

Later on, I eavesdropped as Mum told my fiancé how she always knew I would be a writer, as I was always really good at expressing my feelings in a way that I couldn't do out loud.

She spoke of how I was unable to get the depths of my feelings out of my mouth, especially during an argument. Unable to find the words to explain how I was feeling I'd often end up in tears. I hated it and would run to my room, grab a pen and paper, and let my heart speak. Half an hour later my parents would get a 10-page letter slid under their door (or, if I was especially angry, slammed onto the kitchen counter) explaining what had gone on from all angles and how it made each of us feel. Mum laughed and said, 'We had no idea where she got such emotional understanding from or what to do with it. She thought about things a lot!'

The funny bit is that while Mum had always told me I was 'good with my words,' I didn't believe her. To me a writer was a good speller, a fast reader, top English student, enjoyed reading loads of different types of books, and used a vast vocabulary (*none of which are me*).

However, my whole life I've had a huge guided desire to let my heart speak. Looking back now, it's obvious that writing from my heart and experiencing feelings would be where my path would lead me. But at the time, I had no freaking idea. The dots only make sense when you can join them. But they always join in the end.

WORK YOUR LIGHT

What were you like as a child?

What came easily to you?

What did you struggle with?

How were you different from the other kids?

△

DEVOTE YOUR LIFE

What on earth would you devote your life to if you had the chance? (*You do*). A thing, a cause, lots of things, someone, something you believe in passionately, something that bugs you. Waking up every day. Long hours. Pushing through the hard. Flowing through the good.

What do you do tirelessly even when you're depleted? Especially when you're depleted. What brings you back to life?

What do you do when no one's looking? What do you want to be known for? What one thing do you want to change? What would you still do, if you were the only person left on the planet?

WORK YOUR LIGHT

If you had to devote your life to one thing, what would it be?

THE MEANING OF LIFE IS TO **FIND YOUR GIFT.** THE PURPOSE OF LIFE IS TO **GIVE IT AWAY.**

PABLO PICASSO

△

ASK THE PART OF YOU THAT KNOWS

Who are your heroes? What do they do for a living?

What topic can you never get enough information about?

What are you passionate about?

What comes naturally to you?

What do people thank you for?

What do you love doing more than anything else?

What is your favorite quote?

What annoys you most in the world?

What's your secret dream?

What could you talk about all night long without knowing where the time went?

What would you get out of bed for at 6 a.m. on a Sunday?

If you had to do a TED talk and you knew it would be an awesome success, what would it be about?

What are most of your books about?

If you didn't care what people thought, what would you do?

If you could start your career all over again, what would you do?

If you had five years left before you die, what would you do?

What would you like to be when you grow up?

If you could go back to the day you left school, what would you choose to do for a career?

If your 88-year-old self were giving you advice, what would they say?

If your eight-year-old self were giving you advice, what would they say?

What is your soul calling you to do right now?

What are you going to do about it?

△

WHAT LIGHTS YOU UP?

*'The things you are passionate about are
not random, they are your calling.'*
FABIENNE FREDRICKSON

We light up the world by following what lights us up. What lights you up will be completely different from what lights me up. There are no wrong paths, no whopping mistakes, no complete day-by-day life plan etched into stone by the big G. We are here to share the unique gifts that we all possess. There is no big secret to uncover, no contract which says 'You will do x, after that you will do y, and straight after that you will do z.' We don't discover our soul calling, we uncover it by following the trail of things that light us up and then lose ourselves in the doing.

If you love smelling flowers, smell flowers. If you love writing, start writing. If you love organizing events, put on a show. If you love making art, get out the pastels. If you love raw food, start chopping. If you love taking pictures, snap happy. If you love dancing to classical music with a beat, give me a high kick. Don't feel like you can only do one thing. Give your multi-dimensional soul what it craves. Do them all.

Don't do it for a reason or an end goal, do it because you love doing it. Follow it without knowing where it will lead.

When you follow what you love, the Universe will pick up on your expanded feelings and send you more things to match your newly found expansion.

Following the things that lit me up, I discovered that I loved taking photos, making things beautiful, surrounding myself with nature, but mostly sharing the whispers of my soul through writing. I wasn't writing to tell someone anything, I was writing to feel connected with my soul. I gave myself permission to play with these things every single day (not because I wanted to create something in particular but just because I let myself play).

One day, while walking in Holland Park, I heard my soul whisper and wrote it down in my Moleskine with my favorite black Sharpie. I then took a beautiful photo of me holding the notebook with my big turquoise ring in the shot, and some peonies in the background. I posted the pic onto Instagram along with a bunch of words that came flowing through me. I wasn't writing for someone else, I was writing for myself. I felt light, energized, expanded, and such joy.

So I did it again the next day. And then the next. And then the next. Before I knew it, I had stumbled upon what I now call #RebeccaThoughts, which I post regularly on my social media and blog. Writing these is such a huge pleasure; I could do it for hours and hours on end. When I write them I go into a place where time does not exist, I lose myself and a higher presence steps in. Anyway, #RebeccaThoughts then turned into my free 'Instant Guidance Oracle' on my website.

Over time, after showing up to this joyful practice every day, my own unique writing style started to emerge. And so I wrote every day, for 10 minutes at first, then 20, then 30, then for hours on end. I started getting paid to write channeled #RebeccaThoughts for other people.

I continued to show up and they turned into chapters of this book. What started as a 5-minute bit of play for the pure enjoyment of it is now a full-time job. And it only emerged because I kept following what lit me up without being attached to the outcome.

Start small and follow the invisible trail of the things you love; before you know it you will land smack bang in the middle of your calling.

WORK YOUR LIGHT

So, what lights you up? What do you love doing that
makes you feel joyful, inspired, enthusiastic and light?

1.

2.

3.

4.

5.

6.

7.

8.

9.

10.

Forge out a chunk of time every day to do one of these things, or
maybe even combine them. The trick is to play, don't be attached
to the end point, just enjoy the things that light you up.

FOLLOW WHAT **LIGHTS YOU UP** AND YOU'LL **LIGHT UP THE WORLD.**

△

WILL IT LIGHT YOU UP?

'Run my dear,
From anything
That may not strengthen
Your precious budding wings.'
HAFIZ

Every decision we make either takes us closer or further away from ourselves. Often it's hard to tune in to the subtle energy, but deep down everything is either a 'yes' or a 'no.' Feel good or feel not as good. Brightness or darkness. Avoidance or coming home.

WORK YOUR LIGHT

Next time you are faced with a decision
ask yourself the simple question:

Which solution lights me up?

YOU ARE YOUR HEROES

If there is anything that any human being in all of time has done, you have everything in you to do it too. You are drawn to the people you admire because you recognize something in them that is also in you. That thing you see in the people you admire most is the exact thing that your soul most wants you to express.

One of the biggest 'aha' moments of my life was when I heard Maya Angelou talk about Terence, a playwright from around 150 BC, who wrote.

**I am a human being, I consider nothing
that is human alien to me.**

Up until then I had looked up to my teachers, my heroes, my bosses, and the leaders who came before me with what can only be described as unhealthy admiration. I put them on an unreachable pedestal as if they were above me, as if they had something that I aspired to have... And maybe just maybe if I worked hard enough at embodying the characteristics they had, then one day I might be as good.

But drinking in Maya Angelou's soothing voice I realized that my heroes, phenomenal women – such as Oprah, Sonia Choquette, Elizabeth Gilbert, Miranda MacPherson and Maya Angelou herself – were not separate from me. The reason I admired them was because they actually embodied some of the qualities that I already had deep within my being, I just hadn't allowed myself to express them yet.

They were devoted, courageous, authentic, empathetic, healers, resilient, full of grace, powerful, adventurous, artists, mystics, daring, strong, intuitive, wholehearted, leaders, motherly.

The only difference between them and me was
they were bravely shining their unique light in their ow.
their ego was not in the way. They owned the qualities th.
called to start tapping into. The moment I realized that, the ea
to get out of my own way, to start letting it flow through me an.   it
in a way that only I could.

WORK YOUR LIGHT

Write a list of the five people you admire most, your heroes.

1.

2.

3.

4.

5.

Now write down the three qualities you
admire most about each of them.

1.

2.

3.

These qualities already exist within you.

How can you start expressing them in your life today?

THE WORLD WILL ONLY **ACKNOWLEDGE YOU** TO THE DEGREE THAT YOU **ACKNOWLEDGE YOURSELF.**

△

ACKNOWLEDGE YOU

'It's better to be in the arena, getting stomped by the bull,
than to be up in the stands or out in the parking lot.'
STEVEN PRESSFIELD

You are already all the things that you long to be. Until you stop and acknowledge all that you already are, the world will continue to match your longing for permission with circumstances that delay giving you the go-ahead. All that you dream of, all that you yearn for, and all that you long for, you already are. Sure, some of the things that come along with being that thing may not be present, but that's because we seek a power outside of ourselves to give us permission to be what we already are. Stop wishing, start believing. Live like you already are it (because you are).

If you long to be a writer, it's because you already are a writer. If you long to be an artist, it's because you already are an artist. If you long to be a mother, it's because you already are a mother (regardless of whether you have children or not). If you long to be a healer, it's because you already are a healer. If you long to be a singer, it's because you already are a singer.

Whatever you long for, you already are.

State out loud who you are today. And just show up. Write. Create. Nurture. Heal. Sing. By showing up every day the longing to be expressed will turn into claiming who you truly are, because what yearns to be expressed is who you truly are.

WORK YOUR LIGHT

What do you secretly long to be?
For example, I long to be an artist.

How can you start acting like you already are
it? For example, I will paint every day.

△

THERE'S NO PLACE LIKE HOME

Dorothy's journey in *The Wizard of Oz* is one we all take through life. We search north, south, east, and west only to discover that the very thing we were looking for was inside us all along. The same goes for searching for our callings.

The Scarecrow, the Tin Man, and the Lion all feel they are lacking the one thing that would make them feel whole and purposeful. Scarecrow thinks he doesn't have a brain, Tin Man struggles over his lack of heart, and the Lion believes he doesn't have courage. However, the Scarecrow is actually the smartest of them all, the Tin Man oozes compassion and the Lion has the most courageous heart.

They believe that they must ask the all-powerful Wizard how they can possess these qualities (seeking permission, approval, and validation from an external force). As the journey unfolds it's the exact quality in each of them that gets them to their destination. The Wizard then 'reveals' these traits and their true callings. Scarecrow becomes the wise ruler of The Emerald City, Tin Man a compassionate leader, and the Lion a courageous King.

Often the exact thing we feel we lack is the thing that we already have within us; it's our gift, but our fears are manning the gate.

WORK YOUR LIGHT

What do you think you lack?

Is that true?

△

YOUR GREATEST FEAR IS THE GATEKEEPER TO YOUR HIGHEST CALLING

*'Rule of thumb: The more important a call
or action is to our soul's evolution, the more
Resistance we will feel toward pursuing it.'*
STEVEN PRESSFIELD

Our highest calling is tightly nestled right behind our core fear. As Steven Pressfield says, 'The higher your calling, the more fear you probably have around it.' Annoying but true!

When we step into our biggest, brightest, most expanded self, our core fear is always triggered. Core fears are triggered by a childhood experience, and our ego uses these experiences as evidence that we are separate and alone in this world.

You are not separate. You are not alone.

The ego then creates a script, which plays round and round in our head. By understanding what our ego's script is telling us, we can stop the fear in its track and lessen the power it has over us. Some examples of ego scripts might be:

- 'I'm not good enough.'

- 'I'm bad.'

- 'I'm unworthy.'

- 'I'm all alone.'

- 'There's something wrong with me.'

- 'Everyone abandons me.'

- 'I should be ashamed.'

- 'I'm unlovable.'

- 'I'm nothing.'

- 'It's not safe to be me.'

Which one do you relate to most? Can you track it back to a childhood experience? What's the first time that you recall feeling like this?

The more conscious we are, the less power our core fear and ego's script have on us over time.

My core fear is around rejection with the scripts of 'I'm not good enough' and 'it's not safe to be me.' It was triggered when I was about eight years old after being kicked out of my friendship group at school. What was quite a normal childhood experience had a traumatic impact on me. All of a sudden, the way I saw the world changed and my ego script started playing. Looking back, it's this fear of rejection that caused me to go into my spiritual closet and hold off answering my calling.

And so, when I seriously decided to follow my calling, this fear raised its head – BIG TIME. In fact, any time I answer the call of my soul to expand, I can feel it coming, and a voice in my head saying, 'Hey guuuuurl, who do you think you are?'

But now when it comes I know I'm onto something good. So I let myself feel the fear, state it out loud (either to myself, or even better, a good friend). I then ask my younger self (who first experienced the trauma) what she needs to hear to feel supported.

If you notice your fear coming up, it's actually a good sign that you're stretching yourself in the right direction. If you were playing it safe and ignoring your calling, the ego would have nothing to lose. As you step into your bigness and make the choice to expand, your fears will raise their head.

Think of your fears as *opportunities* to expand, rather than things that are holding you back. If you look at your fears in this light then, as uncomfortable as it might feel, it's actually a sign that you are on the right track.

My teachers always taught me that if you're not uncomfortable, you're probably not growing. And the whole point of us being here is to grow. When fear comes up, give yourself a high five and say 'YES' to expansion.

WORK YOUR LIGHT

Look at the ego script examples (see pages 144–145), and ask, 'What is my core fear?'

Allow yourself to feel that feeling in your body and go back to your first memory of it. It doesn't have to be a conscious memory, it could just be a feeling and an age.

Ask your younger self, 'What do I need to hear to feel safe, loved, and supported?'

Now say this to yourself, as this is probably what you need to hear now.

The next time you feel fear coming up, give yourself a high five and then ask this younger version of you what it needs to feel safe, loved, and supported.

Δ

IF I WASN'T AFRAID I WOULD...

1.

2.

3.

4.

5.

6.

7.

8.

9.

10.

(See all those things? Do them, do them now.)

△

A PRAYER FOR EXPANSION

Beloved Council of Light,

Guide my hands, my heart, my mouth, and my feet.

When I start clinging, remind me to surrender.

When I ignore you, speak up louder than before.

When I make it about me, help me get out of my own way.

When I am fearful, let me see my fears as opportunities to expand.

Thank you for working through me throughout my day.

And so it is.

△

WHAT'S THE WORST THAT COULD HAPPEN?

It's scary to let go of all that we know against the hope of something we want to call in. And it's normal to feel anxious at the thought of letting go of what we know for sure.

So many of my clients tell me that they want to leave their corporate jobs, but are so petrified of leaping that they forget what they are leaping from. When asked, 'What's the worst-case scenario?' their response is generally, 'It won't work out and I will have to go back to this career.'

In other words, if, for some reason, their best possible outcome doesn't work out, the worst possible outcome would involve them being in the situation they're in right now.

They are so scared of the fear of the worst-case scenario that they don't realize that they are actually already in it.

Life bends for the courageous. The Universe wants to support you.

Take a deep breath and leap.

WORK YOUR LIGHT

What are you called to do that scares you?

If you don't do it will you regret it in 10 years?

What's the worst thing that could happen, if you leap?

What's the worst thing that could happen, if you stay put?

△

FIVE PEOPLE

Jim Rohn said, 'You are the average of the five people you spend the most time with.' Which is a pretty powerful statement when you think about it.

Vibrationally speaking, if you have a group of people, the highest vibration and the lowest vibration will always cancel each other out. So, if you are constantly spending time with people who bring you down, you will be brought down. If you are spending most of your waking hours with people who don't take your dreams and beliefs seriously, you are more likely to start doubting them too. Likewise, if you surround yourself with people who think anything is possible, it will rub off.

When we are on the spiritual path, we are in a constant state of growth. This can mean that we outgrow relationships that were once a big part of our lives. When this happens it's hard not to cling on. However, the tighter we try to hold on to people who are no longer an energetic match with the life we are called to live, the further away from our true path and our true selves we stray (and the further they stray from theirs).

Letting go of relationships that no longer serve us doesn't signify a lack of love, rather the opposite. There are times when we need to let go and leave space for new people to come in. Some people come into our lives for a moment, some for a chapter, and some for a lifetime.

If you follow your true path you will never be alone, for it will be filled with people who are walking right alongside you.

WORK YOUR LIGHT

Write down the names of the five people you
currently spend the most time with.

1.

2.

3.

4.

5.

Do these five people represent and encourage your biggest self?

Do they make you expand or contract?

Do they make you feel free or trapped?

Do they inspire you or bore you?

Do they challenge you to grow?

Do they support you?

Are they happy when you win?

Do they believe and value similar things?

Do they encourage you to shine?

Are they aligned with the life you are consciously creating?

△

ASK THE PART OF YOU THAT KNOWS

Right now, if you had to make five guesses as to what your highest calling is, what would you guess?

1.

2.

3.

4.

5.

Circle the one that excites you the most.

If you had to describe this calling in three words, what would they be?

1.

2.

3.

If you had to describe it in one word, what would it be?

△

BLING

If you had $1 million dollars to spend on your calling, what would you spend it on?

If you had $10,000 to spend on your calling, what would you spend it on?

If you had $1,000 to spend on your calling, what would you spend it on?

If you had $100 to spend on your calling, what would you spend it on?

If you had no money but all the time in the world to spend on your calling, what would you spend your time doing?

△

THE UNIVERSE WILL CATCH YOU

The Universe wants to support you, but first you need to leap.

I had known for a good 12 months that I was absolutely definitely going to leave my job in advertising to pursue my calling. I didn't feel ready and the whole thing scared me big time. I had spent way too many sleepless nights trying to work out how I would survive financially, and how I could come out of the spiritual closet in a way that didn't come across too crazy to my peers, who had never seen the complete six-dimensional me. It's not like I wasn't being me, I was just holding parts of myself back.

Being on a three-month notice period, I knew I had to quit my job first and then find part-time work closer to the time. After a couple of failed attempts (*read: chickening out*) I decided to bite the bullet and tell my boss.

I took a deep breath, consciously spoke from my heart to his, and broke the news to him. To my surprise, just five minutes later I walked out of his office with a whopping great grin spread right across my face. Somehow, in the process of following the calling of my soul, I had managed to reduce my working hours to three days a week, get a pay rise, and a promotion.

If that wasn't enough, I was also encouraged to bring my passion into work with possible speaking gigs on creativity and metaphysical marketing combined. So basically I would be paid more to work less and do more of what I loved.

Yes, the Universe has got you covered. It wants to support you. We just need to leap in order for it to catch us. Once landed, our life can become one big stream of flow.

WORK YOUR LIGHT

If you knew the Universe was looking out for
you, what would you do differently?

△

START BEFORE YOU'RE READY

'Forever is composed of nows.'
EMILY DICKINSON

The thing about our calling is that it rarely relies on us taking a leap in a direction that feels a little (*or more likely, a lot*) unknown. It's scary seeing the big gaping hole from where you are and where you long to be, and it's rare to feel ready to leap over it.

I had known for a while that I wanted to teach workshops, but I was sh*t scared to do it. I had no idea where to start and was so afraid of being terrible that I didn't tell a soul about my longing. I prayed for a sign and the next day received a Facebook message from my friend Krish, asking me to take over his intuition workshops in London. I went along and he put me on the spot, leading the group in a meditation. I was nervous and sucked a bit. Something about taking over his workshops didn't feel right, but it was just the push I needed to entertain the idea of doing some myself for real.

A couple of nights later I was at my friend Robyn's house for dinner. An amazing roast chicken and a couple of glasses of wine later, we spoke about the potential of putting on monthly workshops in London. Both of us were craving a down-to-earth community of like-hearted people, so why not create our own!

The next day, we were both at a creativity workshop lead by Julia Cameron. She spoke about the relationship between intuition and creativity (one of my favorite topics) mentioning my mentor and teacher Sonia Choquette, who was coincidentally one of Julia's friends.

As the day progressed, audience members asked Julia to recommend workshops for developing intuition. The whole time Robyn and I were elbowing each other.

At lunchtime we decided that now was as good a time as any to launch our workshops. So we scribbled a note to Julia saying that we ran workshops on intuition and creativity. Julia read the notice out and that day 60 people signed up to attend our workshops. We were in business! (*Little did anyone else know that that was our very first day in business!*)

We put on our first workshop together a month later. One workshop turned into two, which turned into a company called The Spirited Project, which turned into monthly Spirited Sessions, which turned into Spirited Sundays and Spirited Meditation Circles, which turned into events in the UK and Australia, and now we have more planned for Asia and the USA.

What started as a great big fear turned into a wonderful creation, and a lot of fun too. During the first workshop, I was so nervous and afraid of what people were thinking about me that I got in the way of my message. But each time I taught one I became more confident. The more confident I became, the more I enjoyed it. Now I love teaching and leading meditation; thank God I acted before I felt ready and then stuck at it!

If you are called to do something, don't let a little detail like not feeling ready get in the way.

Nobody feels ready the first time they do something. Some people don't even feel ready the first 100 times they do something. Malcolm Gladwell says, 'It takes 10,000 hours to become a master at something.'

The trick is to spend those '10,000 hours' doing things that you feel called to do, rather than becoming brilliant at something you couldn't care less about. No matter in what direction you are being called, if you stick at it, before you know it you will be having the time of your life.

WORK YOUR LIGHT

What are you being called to do that you don't feel ready to do?

What would you be happy to devote
10,000 hours of your life towards doing?

△

JUMP RIGHT ON IN

If you've got a passion, a dream, a goal, some place that you want to leap towards, but are still looking on from afar... Don't freak out looking at all the distance between you and it. Don't wait for permission. Don't just dip your toe in. Instead, jump right on in.

Standing on the outside looking in, with your face all pressed up against the glass, is torture. It's also a waste of your gifts. If you're passionate enough to watch from the sidelines, you will love it even more when you're center stage. That's what you were born for. That's where *you* belong.

Start by making simple daily actions that take you one step closer to being part of the action. Fill your Twitter, Instagram, and Facebook feeds with people already living in that world. Join an online community or reach out to someone who shares the same interest and meet them in person for real. Engross yourself in it all. Start telling people in your life what you're up to, regardless of what you think their reaction might be. Don't hang by the edge. Instead, jump right on in.

WORK YOUR LIGHT

What can you do right now to jump in?

TO EVERYONE ELSE
IT LOOKED LIKE
A SINGLE LEAP.
BUT IN REALITY IT
WAS HUNDREDS OF
LITTLE BABY STEPS.

△

DO ONE THING EVERY DAY

If you do one thing every day towards your calling....

In one year you will have done 365 things.

In two years you will have done 730 things.

In five years you will have done 1,825 things.

In 10 years you will have done 3,650 things.

In 20 years you will have done 7,300 things.

In 50 years you will have done 18,250 things.

Start before you feel ready.

You don't need to know where it's all going.

You'll work it out along the way.

△

JUST DANCE EXTRA QUICK

If you wait until you feel ready you will never ever act. Nobody who has ever done anything considerable waited until everything was perfectly lined up with a guarantee of smooth sailing ahead. That moment simply does not exist.

In 2011, I had just reached my goal of becoming a creative director, and a month later I was on a trip to San Francisco, where I was meant to be working with two terrifyingly senior tremendously talented creatives (who I deeply admired), and I was to direct them. I was way out of my comfort zone, trying to keep my cool while doing the *Wayne's World* 'I'm not worthy dance' in my head.

On my last night there I caught up with my old boss. He had moved from Australia to work for Apple in Silicon Valley. He asked me how it was going and I confessed, 'I have no idea what the hell I am doing and feel like a total imposter the whole time.'

He laughed and gave me the best career advice *ever*. He said, 'Bec, pretty much every day I drive into the car park at Apple I am scared. But then I remember that it's the fear and the challenge that make people great. No one who is doing anything new knows what they're doing. They just work it out along the way.'

Hearing those words from him was exactly what I needed. In one small moment I was able to realize that I wasn't the only one who felt like I didn't know what I was doing and that we are all just working it out as we go along. Even the people I admire most, in fact – especially the people I admire most.

WORK YOUR LIGHT

Pretend you are 88 years old. Write a letter from your 88-year-old self to your current self. What do they want you to go for, to give a shot, to take a big fat leap towards?

What advice do they have for you?

What are they most proud of?

What do they most regret?

LIVE YOUR LIFE TO BEYONCÉ DANCE MOVES.

△

DON'T BE ATTACHED TO THE OUTCOME

Don't be attached to the outcome. Your job is to work out the *what*. The Universe's job is to work out the *how*.

Don't worry about how it's going to pan out, just dive in, and do it with all the love and passion that you can conjure up.

Before you know it, the Universe will surprise you with an outcome that is beyond anything your mind could possibly imagine. But first you need to put your head down and lose yourself in the doing.

When you lose yourself in the doing you invite God in.

△

SHOW UP AND SHINE

From the moment I picked up my first Hay House book I knew I wanted to be an author, but it felt like such a big unachievable dream that I kept it hidden for more than 15 years. Year by year my soul called me more and more loudly. Eventually the nagging got too hard to keep numbing out, so I gave in and just started to write.

I put my heart and soul into a book proposal and sent it off to Hay House with a million prayers and then waited for a response. But I was so focused on the outcome of getting published that I let it paralyze me from actually writing. You see, I wasn't writing for me, I was writing for the approval of a publisher. Focusing on this external outcome stifled my creativity, my ability to write authentically, and share my message. Instead of getting on with writing my book regardless of who picked it up, I was frozen in time, waiting to hear the verdict.

My mentor Sonia said, 'The thing with you Rebecca is that you are waiting for some kind of approval and permission to share your message. You're waiting to be invited to some invisible table, to some imaginary club. There is no table, there is no club. The only approval you need to seek is your own. Don't assume your message isn't relevant until someone else says it is. Don't assume your message isn't relevant until someone else deems it to be. It is relevant. It needs to be told. Stop holding yourself back.'

Tears began streaming down my face as I realized that I had been holding myself back, waiting for some kind of external permission before I shared my gifts. I was seeking approval from an external force that didn't even exist. On the plane back to London, I made a pact with myself. I would stop focusing on getting published and instead focus on showing up to my writing every day.

After all, I love writing; it's what lights me up – why would I wait to do what lights me up? I vowed not to give a f**k what other people thought of my creations. If they didn't like it, well, I'm not for them and they're not for me. So I committed to allowing my message to flow through me as it always had without knowing where it would lead. Regardless of the fear. Especially because of the fear.

So I've decided that it's none of my business who reads my writing, only that I show up and write. It's none of my business, if Hay House publishes this book. Hay House is one path, another publisher is another, and self-publishing another. All I know is that if I don't show up and write, I will feel uncomfortable in my skin, and the niggling feeling and the ache will never let up.

Writing is how I unravel my thoughts. It's none of my business if it's a bestseller, or if only one person reads it. Only that I show up and shine my light. And so, now my affirmation of, 'I am a bestselling Hay House author' has changed to 'I show up and shine my light as far as God sees fit.'

This small shift has changed everything. Since then the writing process has been the most fulfilling experience of my life. I cannot wait to wake up every day, fire up my Mac, and let my soul sing.

It doesn't matter how far our light shines, only that we shine it.

Writing is what fills me up and (like meditation) I am certainly a much nicer person when I sit myself at my desk and do it.

If you have a message that you long to share, don't wait for permission before you act. Dare to follow your highest calling. Let the message in your heart come flooding out. When you devote your life to the things that fill you up and share your message, the Universe can't help but support you. You don't need to know how, just trust that it will.

OMFG!

As I typed the last sentences of the above paragraph, my phone rang. I almost didn't answer it because I was so enjoying writing and the words flowing down through me. When I picked up the phone, I was absolutely speechless to discover Michelle from freaking Hay House on the other end of the phone... offering me a book deal... *Holy sweet Jesus and Mary Magdalene*!

I am still pinching myself. I am humbled beyond measure and doing my best to accept the amazing support that the Universe has for me (and has for us all).

You have a special gift to share. You have a message to tell. You wouldn't be reading this book if you didn't. Don't worry about how. Just show up to it every day and lose yourself in the doing. The Universe *will* conspire to support you. This is something I know for sure.

WORK YOUR LIGHT

How can you show up and shine regardless of the outcome?

Δ

YOU'RE READY

You're ready.

That thing you're called to do.

Do it.

That place you're called to go.

Go there.

Those words you're bursting to say.

Say them.

That dream you've always had.

Live it.

That call deep within your soul.

Answer it.

That thing that lights you up.

Lose yourself in it.

Don't wait until all your ducks are in a row.

Go do it all now.

Don't wait to feel ready.

Just dance extra quick.

It's time.

You're ready.

Go do.

$\triangle$

PERMISSION GRANTED

Permission granted. Go ahead. Please pass go. Start. Begin. Here's the ticket. It's time. We've been waiting. Welcome. Please proceed. Take a seat. Go do. Please progress. Advance. Continue. Enter. Commence. This way. Leap. Kick off. Commence. Do it. Take off. Come forth. Go on. It's about time. At long last. What are you waiting for? You're ready. Let's get this show on the road.

△

MY SOUL IS CALLING ME TO...

Part IV

LIVING
IN THE
LIGHT

Practical tools for
shining your light

WALK WITH YOUR FEET ON EARTH, BUT YOUR HEART IN HEAVEN.

DON BOSCO

△

EMBODYING THE LIGHT

In my twenties, I mentally understood spiritual principles, could put my mind to most things, heard the callings of my soul, and was in touch with my emotions. But I was not embodying any of it. My mind, body, spirit, and soul were working in silos, not flowing in harmony. Like people who live in the same house, but never see each other or socialize, I was not grounding my beliefs in a disciplined way. I wasn't truly living in the flow of it. That was until one of my worst nightmares came true.

Ever since the day I pulled that first Hay House book off the shelf, Louise Hay became my Oprah, Madonna, Beyoncé, Stevie Nicks, and Tina Turner all rolled into one. It was the autumn of 2009 and I was at a Hay House event in London with my friend Julie-Ann Gledhill, who had flown in from Singapore. Reid Tracy (the CEO of Hay House) and Cheryl Richardson were speaking with surprise guest Louise Hay!

At that time in my life I had two feet in advertising, but deep down I knew I had a message to share. In one of the breaks, as everyone else was hanging around forming the 'I love you Louise' club, I was trying to look extremely cool by hanging back. Meanwhile, the whole time I was experiencing the most intense surge of energy racing through my body with a voice from the depths of my soul that beckoned, 'Go ask Louise for a job.' Not normally someone who does that kind of thing, I resisted it.

The next day, the same thing happened. It was as though I was being physically propelled forwards. Unable to resist it anymore, I took a breath, cringing on the inside, cursing my soul, spirit and guides all at once, and made my way to Louise.

Each time she became free, I held back and let someone else go ahead. It was as if my soul and spirit were pushing me, but my body and ego were resisting. The moment the final person started walking away, I took a deep breath and started walking towards Louise, but unable to control my energy literally bowled her over. *OH MY GOD!*

Regaining her balance, Louise then looked me right in the eye and said, 'Girl, don't attack people with your energy.'

I was mortified. My life was definitely over.

While wishing I could disappear off the face of the Earth, I made my way back to my seat and pretended like nothing happened. For the rest of the afternoon I played the situation over and over again in slow motion in my head...

'Was it really that bad?'

Yes, yes it was.

'Did I really bowl over Louise Hay?'

Yes, you did.

Cringe, cringe, cringe...

▽

Later at dinner, I confessed the story to Julie while holding back tears of horrification. Julie thought it was the funniest thing that she'd ever heard, and continues to tease me for it to this day.

Anyway, I tell you that story because it was actually a huge turning point in my journey. I had always been connected to my soul and spirit, received my creative ideas, intuition, and my soul's callings clearly – but I wasn't grounding any of it in my body with action. In other words, my very active mind, body, and spirit weren't talking to each other. So when I heard my soul callings, I didn't embody them with action. And when

I received guidance or creations, I didn't always let it flow through me.

I was receiving all this stuff from the higher realms, but had no idea what to do with it all, so I decided to ignore it. This caused a huge build-up of energy that needed to come out somehow. My mind, body, spirit and soul were not in union. I was out of the flow.

Louise's simple remark sparked a whole new path for me in embodying my spirit and the callings of my soul. Prior to this encounter I thought the mind, body, spirit connection was about strengthening these three parts of us. What this experience revealed is that it is impossible to follow our highest path without energetic integration. And it's difficult not only to hear but *act* on the callings of our soul if we haven't grounded ourselves in regular disciplined practice.

In this new chapter of my journey, I sought spiritual teachers to help me harness the subtle, yet powerful, energies of spirit and anchor them in my body. I have included the ones that work best for me in this section. Try them out and see which ones resonate with you.

SHE'S GOT A **LIGHT** AND SHE KNOWS HOW TO **USE IT**.

△

NON-NEGOTIABLE SPIRITUAL PRACTICE

You cannot hear the callings of your soul if you don't carve time out to listen to them with daily, non-negotiable spiritual practice.

It took me until 2012 to wholeheartedly show up to this practice every day without fail, and it was the best decision I have made. This one thing has created the biggest transformation in my life. Committing to showing up to your soul is like putting a message into the Universe saying, 'I'm serious about this and I'm ready to be supported.'

I used to be a total dabbler. I threw myself into loads of different practices, but I'd often feel overwhelmed with all of the stuff I 'should' be doing. Meditation, journaling, yoga, cutting cords – you name it, I tried it – it felt like I needed a whole extra life to get it all done. And because I didn't have a routine of showing up without fail every day, when I had a super crappy or busy day, my spiritual practice was the first thing to slide. But it was then that I needed my practice the most.

Committing to the discipline of a daily practice doesn't mean you have to meditate for hours or even one, it just means that you show up to something every day without fail. My basic practice takes no more than 20 minutes a day and consists of three things:

1. Light sourcing
2. Prayer
3. Chanting, dance or walking in nature

It is simple (and realistic) enough that no matter where I am or what I've got on, there's no excuse *not* to do it. The more I show up to it, the more my life turns into one big practice, into one big moving prayer.

Whenever a client comes to me wanting change, this is always the first thing I recommend. Your soul is waiting to guide you. The Universe is ready to support you every step along the way. But in order to connect to it, you need to show up.

WORK YOUR LIGHT

Do you currently have a daily spiritual practice
that you show up to every day?

THE QUIETER YOU BECOME, THE MORE YOU ARE ABLE TO HEAR.

RUMI

△

LIGHT SOURCING

My teacher, Sonia, introduced me to Sourcing. I loved it immediately because it is so easy and only took 10 minutes (*which, let's face it, helps*).

From the very first moment I Sourced, I had the most amazing feeling of coming home. It was so familiar. And the craziest thing: I had a sudden memory of Sourcing in bed, or at the beach when I was a little girl, but without even knowing I was doing it!

It's an ultimate prayer of surrender, where you connect back with the universal energy, called 'Source,' and allow yourself to rest, be filled up, and receive all of the gifts that the Universe has for you. Sourcing is a form of daily meditation in which you put yourself into receiving mode so that you can:

- Hear the callings of your soul.

- Remember all of the gifts that you already have within you.

- Connect with the amazing light energy that is on offer to us at all times (but often we look outside of ourselves to find it).

- Nurture your inner light and give it the fuel to shine as bright as humanly possible.

- Be fed by your higher self.

- Let the cosmic energy of the Universe in and surrender to the flow of your highest path.

- Loosen your control on life and let your soul lead the way.

All you need to Source is to open your heart, breathe, and receive. When we Source we open ourselves up to the universal energies of divine love, light, wisdom, and truth. You connect with your higher self and allow yourself to be filled up with whatever it is that you need. It's like taking a drink at the well of your unlimited boundless self. For 10 minutes, you hand over the things that you are striving for, struggling with, trying to heal, and allow yourself to be replenished by the never-ending supply of Source energy.

Let go and relax into the flow of the Universe.

I'm a big believer in morning practice because sleeping is one big meditation and by practicing as soon as we wake up, we maximize this high frequency (rather than reaching straight for our phones).

Most mornings, I walk up to Regent's Park and sit in the rose garden to Source. I love Sourcing in nature, but you can do it from anywhere you like – your bedroom, the bath, your car.

If I have an early morning reading or mentoring session, I light a candle at my altar (see page 208 for creating one of your own) then sit on my meditation stool and Source. But I've also done it on airplanes, trains, buses, even the bathroom, pretty much anywhere I can find to make sure I show up to it each day.

Sourcing is super simple, here's how you do it:

- Rub your hands together to open your heart (your palms are extensions of the heart chakra). Then, gently pull your hands apart and notice the subtle energy you have activated – this is your connection with Source. Rest your hands, palms upwards, on your lap, noticing the subtle pulse that has been activated in the center of your palms.

- Now close your eyes, and imagine a beautiful channel of white light streaming down from the heavens straight for you. Allow this bright supportive light to fill up your entire being and open your heart. Hand over all of your concerns, worries, struggles, goals, hopes, dreams, and any darkness to be replenished by the light.

- Breathe and allow yourself to be supported. Breathe and allow yourself to be filled up. Breathe and allow yourself to be nurtured. Breathe and allow yourself to come home. Breathe and listen to the callings of your soul. Breathe and allow yourself to light up.

- You don't need to worry about your mind being quiet or sitting still for hours, all you need to do is to open your heart, breathe and receive the beautiful energy washing over and into you from the heavens.

WORK YOUR LIGHT

If you haven't already, download the free Sourcing meditation at www.lightisthenewblack.com. Try it for 21 days and watch the transformation. And don't forget to send your Sourcing pics to me, using the hash tag #lightisthenewblack and tagging @rebeccathoughts.

△

LIGHT BATH

You can connect back to Source energy at any moment by giving yourself a light bath – a super quick way to connect and raise your vibration in an instant. Like a mini version of Sourcing (see page 182), a light bath is especially handy for those moments when you find yourself in a low vibe or depleted mood and only have a minute.

Here's how you do it:

- Rub your hands together and, as you do, visualize your heart opening. Then gently pull your hands apart and notice the subtle energy you have activated. This is your connection to Source. Place your hands with palms upwards (in receiving mode).

- Gently close your eyes and imagine a big ball of light from the heavens, shining down endless amounts of light just for you. Imagine the light coming down through the crown of your head straight for your heart and the palms of your hands.

- At the center of your heart, imagine a ball of light. As you receive the light from Source, imagine the ball of light in your heart getting bigger and bigger until it fills your entire being.

- Breathe and receive this beautiful unlimited light energy. Breathe and receive, as it fills you up, replacing any darkness with beautiful luminous light and bringing you back into flow with the Universe.

WORK YOUR LIGHT

Give yourself a light bath.

△

CALL YOURSELF HOME

As we move through our lives, we can leave parts of us behind through trauma, extreme anger, or heartache. The same can happen as we journey from lifetime to lifetime. However, we have the power to call these missing pieces back home, and this meditation is a great tool to do just that.

- Close your eyes and draw your attention to your breath.

- Breathe in for four counts, hold for four counts, and breathe out for eight. Repeat this process three times. Close your eyes and continue to breathe in and out really deeply.

- Now imagine an amazingly powerful magnet at the center of your heart. Breathing in and out, call all the lost parts of you back home. The parts of you lost through traumatic experiences. The parts of you lost through heartbreak, soul ache, and deep disappointment. The parts of you lost through not being truly seen, being under-estimated, and hurt.

- Continue breathing as all of these parts of you are effortlessly pulled back home.

AFFIRMATION

I call all lost parts of me home. I am home. I am home. I am home.

△

BACK TO CENTER

When we are in the flow our energy is balanced. We are not pushing or resisting, we are energetically centered. When we are energetically centered we are ready to receive. My friend Robyn Silverton taught me the following exercise, and it is perfect for getting your energy balanced in an instant. I love it because it takes less than 10 seconds and you can do it absolutely anywhere.

- Stand with your feet flat on the ground. Take a few deep breaths and draw your attention to the soles of your feet, noticing where your weight is. Is it forward in your toes? Or back in your heels?

- If your energy is forward, you are probably stuck in striving, pushing, forcing, controlling, and moving too fast (I used to live here). In this energetic state we are unable to let the Universe (or anyone) help us. We are controlling or giving rather than allowing and receiving.

- If your weight is back in your heels, then you are probably waiting around before you feel ready to act. In this energetic state you are lacking the fire to get up and go, to make stuff happen, to meet people halfway.

- Notice where your energy is without judgment and bring it back to center so that it is equally spread throughout the soles of your feet.

AFFIRMATION

Everything that is calling me is already on its way. I trust that the Universe is doing its part in delivering it all to me. I show up and receive it all.

△

DEAR GOD

*'Every emotion that you feel, good or bad, is about
the relationship between your current thought and
understanding of the Source within you on the same topic'*
ABRAHAM-HICKS

Perhaps you have a great relationship with God/Source/the Universe, or perhaps you were raised to fear God/Source/the Universe. Maybe you were taught that you needed to earn your love, or maybe you were brought up with the mantra that believing in a higher power is a bit airy-fairy.

Whether you have unwavering faith or are a flat-out non-believer, our relationship with, and beliefs about, God/Source/The Universe actually influence so much of how we live our life – especially the things that are left unsaid.

As I demonstrated in Part I with my 'F you God' letter (see page 20), opening up a real dialogue between you and the Source is an extremely powerful tool for interrogating your underlying beliefs and bringing your light into the world.

WORK YOUR LIGHT

Write a letter to God. It might be a F You letter,
a thank you letter, or a simple memo.

Simply write 'Dear God/Divine/the Universe' at
the top of the page and let yourself riff.

Once you're done, take a breath and let God/
the Divine/the Universe respond.

△

IMPROMPTU DANCE BREAKS

We all receive intuitive guidance, but most of us wait for that guidance to make sense before we act on it. Our mind, body, and soul are disconnected.

A wonderful way to embody your soul is through dance. Intuitive movement is the act of moving your body, however it feels like moving, letting your soul and spirit dance you. It might be gentle swaying, or some Sister Act style deep-shoulder action... Whatever your style, this simple act of letting your soul move you serves the following purpose:

- It strengthens the right hemisphere of the brain, which is linked to your subconscious, intuitive, and creative mind.

- It allows your body to process any stuck energy and emotions so you can get back in flow, and so is great if you're feeling stuck or down.

- It allows your soul to lead your body – physically rewiring your brain – so that you're more inclined to let the callings of your soul (your intuition) truly lead your life.

WORK YOUR LIGHT

Throw your own dance party for one. It need not take ages, one song will do. Close the door, crank up the music, close your eyes, and let your soul move your body. The more you move your body in ways it has never moved before, the more effective it will be in releasing old patterns.

△

TAKE A BREATH

'Fear is excitement without breath.'
ROBERT HELLER

It's the easiest and most natural part of life. So many of us go about our day taking shallow sips without air even reaching our bellies. Take a moment now to notice what your breath is doing right now. Is your breathing deep or shallow? Take a huge breath in and let it fill the depths of your belly.

To breathe deeply is to gulp in life. To breathe consciously is to say to the Universe, 'I am here and I am ready to receive.'

Do not underestimate the healing potential of the simple action of taking a breath. My teacher Sonia stressed to me the importance of breath, but it wasn't until all I could do was breathe that I fully understood.

When I was at my lowest point, proper rock bottom, I went to a shamanic healer I had been seeing for a while. I was in such extreme grief that my body simply didn't want to breathe. My soul had almost given up. As I was lying there, she instructed me to take a breath. My brain was desperately instructing me to do it, but it was like my spirit had packed up shop and left. I would go about 20 seconds until I took a breath, and then it would be the shallowest of sips, just enough to survive until the next baby breath.

The truth was, I did not want to be here anymore. I was too tired and devastated to keep going. I had fought too hard for too long and I couldn't pretend any longer that everything was all right. So we spent the whole session literally trying to get me to breathe. Little by little

I could feel my spirit coming back home. After about 30 minutes my chest started to rise, and a week later I allowed air back into my belly.

But you don't have to be at rock bottom to notice the impact of your breathing. If you feel stuck, tired, stressed, or afraid... just change your breath. It brings in the life force and gets things moving. Just like a good spring clean does to your house, breathing in deeply can transform any stagnation or stuck energy.

WORK YOUR LIGHT

With your hand on your belly, take 60 seconds right now to pay attention to your breath.

Is it slow and deep, rapid and shallow, or perhaps you are holding it? Notice the difference between your inhalations and your exhalations.

Begin to take in more air, pulling it deep into the corners of your belly, right down into your feet.

Δ

WHO LIGHTS YOU UP?

You've worked hard to raise your vibration, so it's worth taking note who in your life raises you up energetically and who drains you.

This doesn't mean that you should only hang out with people who are committed to raising their frequency and in an optimistic place in their lives. Rather, it's about becoming aware of who has the tendency to drain you, so you can protect your energy and decide on how much time you spend with them.

Who makes you feel good and who makes you feel bad?

As we raise our vibration and shift energetically, we may find that we want to spend more time with people who are on a similar path. Or at least look at protecting our energy when hanging around those who drain us.

WORK YOUR LIGHT

Who in your life drains you and leaves you feeling depleted?

Is there anyone in your life that you take energy
from, instead of sourcing it from within?

△

WHERE'S YOUR ENERGY AT?

The higher your vibration, the more energetically sensitive you are likely to be. Protecting your energy is imperative to prevent yourself from being energetically depleted.

Here are some super, simple ways to protect, replenish and clear your energetic field.

Protect your energetic field

It is important to protect our energetic field in order to hear our intuitive voice clearly and prevent our vital energy from being drained by people and life in general. You can do this by imagining a protective energetic space about 1 metre (3 feet) around you, which nobody can penetrate without your permission.

Chakra shower

Chakras are wheels of energy in and outside the body. Each chakra point is associated with different emotions and bodily functions. As we go about life, our chakras can become blocked or stagnant. Giving yourself a chakra shower is a simple way of clearing your energy each morning while you are in the shower. Simply scan each of your chakras one by one, noticing anything that is blocked in each of them. As the water runs over your body imagine it cleansing away any energy that is stuck or stagnant in each of your chakras. At the end, call upon the light of Source energy to fill each of them up with luminous white light.

Cutting cords

Cords are the invisible energetic connection between two people. Attached to a chakra in each person, the cord feels more like a hook, and is generally controlling and manipulative. A healthy relationship is two whole people coming together, therefore it is important to cut the energetic cords that pop up as we move through life.

At the end of each day, tune in to your body and notice if there is anyone who is tugging at you energetically. In your mind's eye, scan each of your chakras and notice where the cord is attached to you and what the cord seems to be made of.

Perhaps it's a hook, a rope, a ribbon, or maybe even a steel cable. Imagine cutting this cord with a pair of scissors, or some other tool. If you need extra help doing this, call upon Archangel Michael with his big silver sword to do the cutting with you. At the end imagine a ball of white light protecting you.

Light bubble

Imagine your entire body being protected by a giant bubble of bright white light. This bubble is impenetrable by anyone or anything, protecting you every step of every day.

Earthing

Magic happens when we experience a complete union of mind, body and spirit. If we are not grounded and in our body, it is difficult to let our intuition move us, we are likely to feel unsupported by life and we run the risk of staying too much in thought rather than action. Earthing is a wonderful way to ground and embody our mind, body and spirit. It's super easy to do and can be done absolutely anywhere.

Find yourself a patch of earth (or if you can't find earth just imagine it) and stand with your shoes and socks off. Really feel the texture of the earth beneath your feet.

Send any blocked energy or emotions you are struggling with to the Earth through your right foot. Through your left foot, allow the healing frequency of the Earth to send you positive healing energy, and let it flow through your entire body.

High five a tree

Just like Earthing, you can transmute bad energy just by touching a tree. Place your hands on the trunk of a tree, and ask it to charge you up and help you dissolve any bad energy you may be holding.

Epsom salt baths

Soaking in an Epsom salt bath is not only a great way to protect and cleanse your energetic field, they're also brilliant for detoxifying your body and soothing your adrenal glands. I have one several times a week and feel so balanced after.

Note: If you have a heart condition, are pregnant, or are on any medication check with your medical practitioner before using Epsom salts.

LIGHTHOUSES DON'T GO RUNNING ALL OVER AN ISLAND LOOKING FOR BOATS TO SAVE; THEY JUST STAND THERE SHINING.

ANNIE LAMOTT

△

BE THE LIGHTHOUSE, NOT THE ELECTRICITY

As a Lightworker your purpose is to 'be the light.' Being the light does not mean that you become the light source for others by plugging yourself into them energetically.

Being the light means turning your light on, so that you can be the light, not be *their* light. Only they can be their light. As you connect with your own light source, you then effortlessly light up the way for others to connect with theirs.

You cannot fix or save anyone who doesn't want to be fixed or saved. If you assume other people are helpless, then you are actually doing them a disservice by taking away the opportunity for them to turn on their own light and be in flow with the Universe themselves.

WORK YOUR LIGHT

Are you running around 'looking for ships to save' or are you focusing your attention on simply shining bright like a lighthouse?

SHE LIT UP
EVERY ROOM.

△

SACRED SOCIAL

How we interact on social media contributes to the future consciousness of the world. Our likes, shares, posts, pics, pins, and tweets; all of it is energy and it is being constantly cast out into the ether – and then multiplied over and over again at the speed of light.

In every moment, we can consciously choose what energy we contribute: The words don't matter, but the energetic intent behind them does. Just as your thoughts create your world, our collective energy creates THE world. Thanks to social media, this collective energy can now spread even more quickly – which is why it's important now more than ever to watch your thoughts and be intentional with the energy you bring.

Check in on the intent that you are putting out there as you post. Do you want to share your light, encourage the light in someone else, or is it coming from another place?

The more we put our physical energy toward the things that are in alignment, the more that vibration and level of consciousness will spread. So if you see a post that resonates with you, like or retweet it.

The magnificent thing about this period of history we are living in is that we can use the instant infinite power of social media to help us share and spread our messages. Regardless of whether you are using social media for your own personal use or for your business, it has the same power.

WORK YOUR LIGHT

Get sacred with social media by practicing intentional posting.

△

CHOOSE A HIGHER THOUGHT

We all have bad days and sometimes crap things just happen. You can't change the situation, but you can change the way that you think about it.

The worst thing you can possibly do, when you find yourself in a negative mood, is to berate yourself for being in a negative mood because you are meant to 'be the light.' We're human, human emotions are normal.

Let yourself feel whatever you need to feel, and then, when you're ready, choose a higher thought. It doesn't matter if it's only a teeny bit higher.

Baby steps are better than no movement at all.

WORK YOUR LIGHT

The next time you're feeling a bit meh, feel the feelings, breathe, and choose a higher thought.

△

CREATE A VIBRATION BOARD

In order to attract something into our lives, we need to be a vibrational match. If we continue to focus on it as something we want 'in the future,' that thing will always remain 'in the future.'

I've had success with vision boards, but there were always some things that I could never quite become a vibrational match for. Then I had an idea, to combine the following things together:

- The things we're calling in (what we want).

- The things we've already called in (what we've already attracted).

- The things that light us up (what we love).

When we bring our future wants into alignment with what currently is, our brain cannot distinguish between the two and so it's much easier to become a vibrational match, thus helping us attract it more quickly.

I call it a 'vibration board.' It's a vision board + a feel-good board.

So, alongside the convertible, the beach house, my affirmation – 'I shine my light as far as the Universe sees fit' – and meeting Oprah (of course), I have pictures of the people I love the most, pictures of me with my teachers, articles written about me, and a love letter from my fiancé. So my feel-good moments are mixed up with my future manifestations.

WORK YOUR LIGHT

Create your own vibration board filled with the things you are calling in, have already successfully called in, and that light you up!

△

MAKE YOUR LIFE A MOVING PRAYER

I've never been big on the formalities of going to church, but ever since I was a little girl I've had an unshakable knowing that God exists. I'm not talking about a big man in the clouds, rather an unknown presence that connects us all.

My mum taught me to pray at an early age, and I have done it ever since. I never really even knew who I was praying to, but I always felt I was being heard. The act of reaching out and connecting from my heart to the heart of the Universe made me feel more supported and connected to life as a whole. While my body was here on Earth, my heart was always in heaven and praying always reminded me of that.

Prayer and meditation go hand in hand. If you want to ask for something, pray. If you want to listen to the answer, meditate. There have been times in my life when my prayer and meditation practice dissipated. Looking back, these were the times that I felt most separate and alone in the world.

Nowadays I choose to keep the conversation (asking and listening) going at all times, so my life is one big moving prayer.

You don't need to get on your knees to pray, you can do it while you are walking down the street, washing the dishes, filing your nails, giving a presentation, or riding your bike. It can be a simple chat, a plea for help, an expression of gratitude, a request for guidance, or putting in your order for what you'd like to experience next.

Prayer doesn't have to be reciting words out loud. It can be thoughts and wishes, cries and silence, confessions and requests, gratitude and wonder. It is merely a reaching out to something beyond our separate human self.

In her book *Help, Thanks, Wow*, Annie Lamott speaks of the three main types of prayer.

1. **Help:** When we are brought to our knees and admit we need help.

2. **Thanks:** A moment of gratitude when we receive the help and realize that our prayers have been heard.

3. **Wow:** When the miraculous beauty of life takes our breath away.

When we make our life one big moving prayer, we move into a space of constant connection. There is no space that prayer begins and ends. We are in constant communion with life itself.

WORK YOUR LIGHT

Create your own prayer practice and make your life a moving conversation with something beyond your separate human self.

△

YOUR SPIRIT GUIDES ARE WAITING

You have a team of spirit guides waiting to support you. The only catch is that they cannot help you unless you ask them to. You can do this in an instant. You can do this right now.

Spirit guides are beings from the sixth dimension and above, and are completely devoted to your growth. Many have had lifetimes here on Earth and just like you they have their own eclectic bundle of gifts, wisdom, and experiences. They have been carefully chosen just for you. Perfectly suited to your highest calling, their only job is to support you and guide you as much or as little as you wish.

In giving soul readings, I have found that most people have approximately six guides in their inner circle and we call in new ones, as we need them.

We are born with spirit guides and we can also recruit them as we move through life. They can guide you through anything from finding a car park to healing your heart, from experiencing more joy to finding the right job, from meeting your future partner to getting through your darkest hour. No request is too big or too small, too specific or too broad.

If you are undertaking a particular creative endeavor, for example, you might recruit a spirit guide who has written books of their own during their time on Earth. If you are going through a particularly hard time you could call on a wise teacher guide to help you through it.

I have been working with my spirit guides half-heartedly for a number of years and the truth of the matter is that I spent a long time waiting for them to appear in black and white before I took them seriously.

I wanted a personal relationship, to see and feel them like I would a friend or family member. I wanted to know their age, their background, their personality, and hair color. I wanted them to pop over for dinner and share a bottle of red.

I would get hunches and the odd vision in my mind's eye, but would quickly dismiss it thinking I had no proof. After confessing this to my teacher a couple of years ago, I was guided into a meditation where I agreed to be open to experiencing them without any expectations. To my surprise, by letting go of what I thought this experience should look like, each of my spirit guides came to me.

One is a woman called Charlotte. She is a terribly English high-society lady from the 1920s, here to help me get my message and name spoken about in the right circles; a gifted gossip, with her fingers in all of the most influential of pies.

Knowing that I wanted some publicity to increase my chances of being published by Hay House, I asked my spirit guide Charlotte for help. That same day I was connected with a journalist called Anita Chaudhuri. One week after that a story landed on Anita's desk about British Spirituality for the *Sunday Times Style Magazine* (which also happened to feature several Hay House authors). Three days after that she got another feature story in *Psychologies* magazine. Anita interviewed me for both.

When I went to meet the Hay House team for the first time, they asked for the name of my publicist. Without thinking, I responded, 'My spirit guide Charlotte.' Everyone around the table burst into laughter. I've sat at a lot of boardroom tables in my life, but that was the first where I could have mentioned my spirit guides. How awesome is that?!

WORK YOUR LIGHT

Want to meet your spirit guides? Download my guided meditation at www.lightisthenewblack.com

△

INVEST IN YOUR SOUL'S GROWTH

Your soul is your most valuable asset. You can lose everything in a second, but nobody can take your soul growth away from you.

The biggest blessings you can share with the world are your light, your love, and your consciousness (*they're all the same thing to me*). You are here to grow as a soul and help the consciousness of the planet grow in the process. As you expand, so does the Universe. For whenever you are investing in your own expansion, you are investing in the expansion of the Universe. If you ask me, anything that can bring you closer to your potential, to your spirit, to your true essence, is priceless.

I have spent huge amounts of money, time, and effort on my personal soul growth. Books, courses, healers, training, retreats, trips, pilgrimages, mentoring, coaching, shamans, CDs, websites, making difficult decisions, taking leaps of faith, and more. But you know what? Each time I have invested in my soul's growth, I received that amount back plus tenfold more.

WORK YOUR LIGHT

How are you being called to invest more in your soul's growth?

△

ASSEMBLE YOUR SUPPORT TEAM

We are pack animals, we are not meant to go it alone. Everyone needs a support team, people who have your back no matter what and encourage you unconditionally. They're the ones who are genuinely as happy as you are when things go well. And feel it hard when things don't go quite to plan. They hold your vision and keep you on the right path. They are standing by, a phone call or a flight away ready to have your back the moment you say the word.

The space around you is sacred, so treat it accordingly. If you haven't already started, begin assembling your support team. Who you hire is completely up to you but it's the most important job spec you'll ever write.

The most amazing people in history have all had theirs: Jesus and his disciples, Obama and the White House, Kylie and her sexy back-up dancers.

It may consist of friends and family, teachers and healers, psychics and shamans, neighbors, peers and pets – it doesn't matter how many or how few. All that matters is that they are there to support you and, no matter how bright or how dark the day, they will be there to cheer you on.

WORK YOUR LIGHT

Assemble your support team. Write the names of five to 10 people who support your dreams unconditionally. If you can't think of that many people, then send a request out to the Universe to start sending them to you today.

△

MAKING AN ALTAR

Creating an altar in your home is a really effective tool for anchoring your spiritual energies into the physical. A sacred space filled with things that make you feel connected. Think of it as a little corner of the world where you can come to hope, dream, wish, pray, meditate, contemplate, and ask the Universe for support.

- Start by choosing a place for your altar. If you live with others and it's hard to find personal space, you can make yours a portable one consisting of just a candle and a special object, such as a crystal, which you keep on your bedside table. You can make your altar on a window ledge or it can take up the whole corner of a room. Size does not matter, intention does.

- Choose sacred items that make you feel connected and full of light. Consider what you want to call in. You might have a candle, a picture of a god, goddess, or guru that means something to you, incense, fresh flowers, a lucky charm, angel cards, artwork, magazine clippings, feathers, a champagne cork, a picture of a loved one. There are no rules, just choose whatever makes your soul feel good.

- Your altar is a place where you can go to pray, meditate, ask for support and set your intentions for the day. You might want to light a candle and say a prayer, such as 'Please Use Me' (see page 223) after Sourcing.

- The altar is an energetic portal for you to communicate with the Universe, so it's important to maintain it and keep it fresh. You may feel guided to replace things now and then, or even pick a flower each week to keep the energy clear and sacred. Don't overthink it; just go with what feels good.

WORK YOUR LIGHT

Make yourself an altar. If you've already got one, post your pics using #LightIsTheNewBlack.

Δ

LEAVE SPACE FOR GRACE

If we fill up our lives right to the brim, then there is no space for the new to come in. If your life is cluttered, the Universe has nowhere to deliver the new things that you are praying for.

Doing a regular physical de-clutter of your life can help let go of the things that no longer serve you, making way for the new. As you throw away old boxes from the past, you are also letting go of old thought patterns, and fears.

When we hold on tightly to the things around us, we are so busy clinging on that we are unable to catch the things that are coming straight for us.

Letting go and leaving a little bit of space wide open is scary, but that's why everyone doesn't do it.

You're not everyone. You are courageous.

And I reckon, there's something you're ready to let go of to make way for something even better that you truly deserve.

WORK YOUR LIGHT

If you weren't afraid of something not taking
its place, what would you let go of?

△

MY SOUL IS CALLING ME TO...

Part V

BE
THE
LIGHT

Serve the world by being you

TRAVEL LIGHT, LIVE LIGHT, SPREAD THE LIGHT, BE THE LIGHT.

YOGI BHAJAN

△

YOUR LIGHT IS NEEDED HERE

Do not underestimate the power your light has in creating change in the world. Your light shines brightest when you bravely step up into your biggest most authentic self. You will never know the true extent of your impact, but you can trust that it will be more than you could ever fathom. Your light is needed here.

△

YOU DO YOU (#YDY)

Don't waste your time striving to become the person you
long to be, spend your time being the person you already
are. The person you long to be is already inside you.

You do YOU.

Say you long to be a writer. If you long to be a writer it
means you already are one. You don't need someone to
come along and confirm it's true, grant your wish, or give
you approval. It's who you are. Already, right now.

You do YOU.

When we spend our time being who we already are, the
doing ends up being a byproduct of the being. So if you're
a singer, go be that regardless of the outcome. It's who
you are. You don't need to do anything in order to be
it some day. She's in you. She wants to sing now.

You do YOU.

It's none of your business how many people read your
books or download your songs or compliment your latest
design, or buy your art or like your page or retweet your
tweet. What is your business is showing up to what lights
you up, to what makes you come alive, to that which makes
your light shine even brighter. Let go of your attachment
to the outcome. It's none of your business anyway.

You do YOU.

It's the most fantastic thing when you simply focus on the being and
do from there. Any attachment to the outcome magically disappears

and something very special happens... by allowing yourself to be filled up by the being, the Universe can't help but support you.

You do YOU.

So go be YOU, regardless of the outcome. Go do the things that you love, regardless of how good people think you are. Without even bothering your head about what others say.

You do YOU.

You already are all the things you strive for. And the more you show up to who you already are, the more filled up you become. The more filled up you become, the more YOU you become. The more YOU you become, the brighter you shine for all those around you.

You do YOU.

△

THE WORLD NEEDS YOU

If you follow what you love, while doing it in a way that only you can, you will serve the world by being you. If you spend your time trying to be like someone else, you will be holding back the unique gifts that only you can bring.

In her Dartmouth commencement address, Shonda Rhimes (writer of *Grey's Anatomy* and my all-time favorite TV writer) talked about how when she left college her dream was to BE Nobel Prize-winning author Toni Morrison. Eventually she realized that the role was already taken and the world certainly did not need another one. The only role available for her to be was Shonda Rhimes. So she followed what lit her up, went to film school, and wrote stories in a way that only she could.

Many years and Golden Globes later, in one of those glorious full-circle moments, Shonda Rhimes then finds herself sitting opposite Toni Morrison at dinner. And all her idol Toni Morrison wanted to talk about was what was happening in *Grey's Anatomy... I LOVE that!*

Shonda explained it so beautifully when she said, 'That never would have happened if I hadn't stopped dreaming of becoming her [Toni Morrison] and gotten busy becoming myself.'

Her dream didn't come true. Something even better did. She became herself instead.

The best possible outcome that the Universe has planned for you is way better than the biggest dream you could ever imagine. The trick is to lose yourself in following the things that light you up and do it in a way that only you can.

**The world needs your presence. Serve
the world by being you.**

WORK YOUR LIGHT

Are you striving to be like someone you admire, or more like you?

△

BEING OF SERVICE

'I've learned that people will forget what you said, people will forget what you did, but people will never forget how you made them feel.'
MAYA ANGELOU

Being of service means devoting your life to something greater than yourself, so that your presence can make a difference in the world.

Being of service doesn't have to be a humongous mission where you need to singlehandedly save the world, cure cancer, or run off to a Buddhist monastery. Making a difference in just one person's life can have immeasurable ripples.

My year seven English teacher Ms. Dorothy Bottrell served the world by embracing her eccentricity, open-heartedness, and presence, and by encouraging creative uniqueness in all of her students. Instead of wearing something plain and simple, like all the other teachers, every day her outfit was an expression of her spirit. When she spoke to her students, she spoke to their hearts and made them feel truly seen. From the first day that she took roll call, I felt both special and inspired all at once.

Ms. Bottrell turned a creative writing assignment into an inspiring adventure. She told us that there were stories waiting to be told and that we were the perfect people to tell them. She informed us that our assignment was not to write a piece of creative writing; it was to write our very first book. And the reward for writing the book was to be able to share our creations with the children at the local kindergarten.

She said that these children were waiting for us to tell them the story that only we could tell!

Ms. Bottrell inspired me to pour my heart and my soul into my book, *Where do Rainbows Come From?* In school vacations I went to secondhand bookstores looking for ancient inspiration from all of the ages and mystic traditions. I spent hours illustrating it with my favorite Derwent watercolor pencils. It was even 'published' by Tucker Glynn & Co. – my friend Terri's dad's accounting firm had a color printer and binding machine (*hey, it was the nineties*).

I will never forget the day when Ms. Bottrell handed back our books and congratulated us for being 'authors.' Enclosed with my book was a handwritten two-page letter straight from her heart with a carefully chosen wrapped present of a rainbow and dolphin window sticker and a poem written by her that she said was inspired by my story. I started crying from how special and loved I felt in that moment. I then looked around the room and discovered that she had written a letter and carefully chosen a present for every student in the class.

Ms. Bottrell had touched the hearts and encouraged the spirits of every single one of us. I still have my book and, in the process of writing this one, got my mum to bring it over to me when we met up in Paris.

Ms. Bottrell was completely unconventional, and unlike any other teacher I have ever known. Had she spent her years striving to be like someone else, the world would be a much less compassionate, creative, and bright place. My life for one would have been a little different and I have no doubt that there are hundreds if not thousands more who were touched by her spirit.

MANTRA

I light up the world by being me.

SERVE WHERE YOUR HEART SWELLS.

△

PLEASE USE ME

I request the Grace of the Universe to work through me
today so that I can serve the world by being me.

Let my light shine as bright as the Universe sees fit and
touch the hearts of those who need it most.

May my life be one big moving prayer.

Amen.

△

YOU©

You are like no other in this town, city, country, continent, planet, solar system, galaxy, Universe, Multiverse, and beyond. Way beyond. Through all the dimensions of space and time, there is, never has been and, never will be anyone quite like you. Not even close. Your hair color, your upbringing, your highs and your lows. Your accent, your nature, and all the lessons you've learned along the way. Your body size, your skin color, and all the learning from the lives that your soul has swum through before. You are a glorious tapestry that is being woven with every new breath. Evolving with every thought and every act and every moment.

Now, now, now.

In the entire existence of all the humans that ever were and ever will be, none will come close to possessing the same combination of amazingness that you have right now. You are the gift. You are the light. It's your You that lights up the world. Be like no other.

Be You©.

FORGE,
DON'T FOLLOW.

△

FORGE, DON'T FOLLOW

The age of worshiping and playing follow the leader is over.

Simon says You do You (#ydy).

There is also no one on this planet that comes even close to possessing the same combination of unique skills, gifts, life experience wrapped up in the same package as you. Fact.

If you spend your time striving to be like someone else five things will happen:

1. You will do a second-rate job doing what someone else will always do better, and more quickly, effortlessly, and naturally.

2. By the time you work out how to do it their way, they will have evolved and moved on to their next fabulous thing.

3. Your success will be limited because you will be out of flow with the Universe.

4. You miss creating your own unique masterpiece and lighting up the world with your presence.

5. Being out of flow with the Universe, things will always feel a little hard.

Don't look to the people who have come before you to work out your way, forge your own path. We do this by embracing our complete 360-degree self (*weirdness and contradictions are good things*).

It takes courage, but once you are on your way it feels absolutely fantastic because – everything works in perfect harmony – it fits, everything is built around your You. And before you know it, chances are, your path will roll up alongside those who you once admired and they will admire you for forging your own.

WORK YOUR LIGHT

What one thing can you do today to forge
your own path courageously?

$\triangle$

EMBRACE YOUR WEIRD

*'You're mad, bonkers, completely off your head. But
I'll tell you a secret. All the best people are.'*

ALICE IN WONDERLAND, LEWIS CARROLL

The dictionary meaning for weird is 'extraordinary, out of this world.'
Don't know about you but I'm all in for that! Don't be normal. Embrace
your weird. Get naked. Release your inner oddball. Let your crazy out.
When you do, three amazing things happen.

1. The people in your life who don't really love you for you will drop
    away. This might feel like a loss but really it's a win.

2. You will feel a hell of a lot more fantastic and free. Oh, and you will
    be on your way to serving the world by being Y*O*U.

3. You will clear the space for your people to find you. The kinds of
    people who are actually looking for the exact thing that you already
    are.

By embracing my 'weirdness' – in other words coming full throttle out of
the spiritual closet and proudly owning it – I attracted my fiancé Craig.
He says that the moment he walked into my bedroom (full of crystals,
angel cards, sage sticks, pendulums, and books on the Akashic records)
he knew I was going to be his future wife.

I later found out that when he was growing up all his friends thought he
was 'weird' because instead of having a poster of Kylie Minogue above
his bed he had Sabrina the teenage witch!

Weird is the new normal. Let's weird it up!

△

MY WEIRDNESS LIST

1.

2.

3.

4.

5.

6.

7.

8.

9.

10.

△

CALL IN YOUR PEOPLE

*'We are all a little weird and life is a little weird, and when we
find someone whose weirdness is compatible with ours, we join
up with them and fall in mutual weirdness and call it love.'*

Dr. Seuss

Call in your people. They're out there.

The ones that get you.

The ones who are the same kind of bonkers as you, the same kind of weird.

Those you don't need to explain anything to.

Who want you to win and feel it when you fall.

Who light up when they see you.

Who, no matter how long they've been on the planet, feel like they've spent all of it looking for you.

They're out there. And they want to find you. But you gotta lean into your weirdness, so they know it when they see you.

WORK YOUR LIGHT

Who do you already have in your life that is one
of your people, the same kind of weird?

How can you embrace your weirdness to
call in more of your people?

THEY WERE THE SAME KIND OF **WEIRD**.

△

LET YOUR SPIRIT BE YOUR BRAND™

I spent over a decade in advertising helping some of the world's biggest brands find their authentic voice. Brands throw millions into carefully curating what you have right now. What no person or thing can take away or come close to impersonating.

The whole process of branding is personification. Because brands aren't born with a unique spirit (unlike you), their spirit must be manufactured. Establishing a brand for a product is the process of quite literally creating a personality, set of beliefs, tone of voice, and visual style that did not exist prior to creating it.

You were born with your own personal brand; you might not have known it, but it existed in full the moment you took your first breath. But it didn't begin there. You've been curating it for maybe hundreds, thousands, perhaps even millions of years. It's living and breathing in a constant state of evolution. It's your essence, your spirit, your You-ness.

It's You©

It's in there. And it wants to come out. Now it's just a matter of identifying, remembering, and choosing to bring it out into the light of day. It's you at your most expansive. The You, which is bursting to be released. The shining, sparkling, powerful You.

We expand when we allow ourselves to embrace, own, and express the unique wonder of who we truly are. We retract when we turn our back on our magnificence by trying to be more like someone else. When we retract, we go against Source and the flow of the Universe.

Choose to expand and let your spirit be your brand.

WORK YOUR LIGHT

List ten words that describe You best. Your You-ness.
Your You©. Beyond what society has said about you
and the roles you play. Who you really are.

1.

2.

3.

4.

5.

6.

7.

8.

9.

10.

If you had to condense it down to five words, what would they be?

1.

2.

3.

4.

5.

If you had to condense it down to three words, what would they be?

1.

2.

3.

△

YOUR TRIBE'S WAITING FOR YOU

'We need you to lead us.'
SETH GODIN

The world needs more leaders. More people who can courageously step out, speak up, and guide the way. You don't need to have it all together to lead. In fact, it helps if you don't. No one wants a perfect angel who hasn't made any mistakes.

Let your life be your message. Don't underestimate the power of sharing your story. It's through hearing someone else's journey that we feel less alone. We can see that if there was a way out for them then there may be a way out for us too. We realize that we are actually all in this thing called life together.

We are not as alone as we feel.

The difference between a follower and a leader is that the leader has the courage to go first. In bravely stepping out, they shine a light on the path for others to venture forward, too. Don't fret too much about trying to work out who your tribe is. Don't get stuck in age, income level, hobbies, and occupation. The best way to discover your tribe is actually to look in the mirror. If you feel called to lead, chances are it is because at some point in your life you longed for someone to lead you. Your tribe is longing for exactly the same thing as you were (and are).

Your tribe might only be one step behind you. Hell, they might even be right alongside you. You don't need your ducks in a row or a special certificate to give you permission. The only thing you need is the courage to stand up. Embrace your struggles, the peaks, and the troughs. You don't need to know the way. Just that you believe that there might be a different one.

Your tribe is waiting for you. Step forward so they can find you.

WORK YOUR LIGHT

At what point in your life did you most long for someone to lead you?

Looking back, what did you most need to hear from someone then?

△

YOU ARE YOUR MESSAGE

Your message is your life. Your struggles and your triumphs. Your highs and your lows. Your start and your middle. There is no end.

It's the things you are most proud of and the ones you'd rather forget. And the more specific your story, the more universal your message.

Regardless of how you choose to spread your light, it will touch more people when you allow yourself to be transparent about your journey and the hardest lessons learned along the way. The good and the bad. The best teachers are eternal students; their message grows as they do.

Your message is the moral of your story. And there are people waiting to hear it. A story left unsaid is the saddest story of them all. Share yours now.

WORK YOUR LIGHT

A great way of getting clear on your message is to imagine it to be a Hollywood movie. It doesn't need to be your entire life story; it could just be a chapter. Ask yourself:

What would the movie be about?

What genre is it?

What would the main character be like?

What about the supporting roles?

Who/what is the antagonist?

What is the moral of the story?

What's the title?

▲

CHOOSE YOUR OWN THEME SONG

Choosing your own theme song is an awesome way to stay connected to who you truly are. Think of it as a musical anchor to call yourself home, light you up, and give yourself a pep talk. You can play it every morning when you wake up, while you're strutting down the street, before an important meeting, or to bring you back on track when you're in a bad mood.

Your theme song can be absolutely anything you choose it to be. If you want to get creative you can even make up your own. I've been playing my own theme song (*She's a Rainbow* by the Rolling Stones) for a few years now. At first I chose it because it embodied everything that I longed to become (which was who I was at my core), but felt too self-conscious to reveal. Each time I played it, it was almost like calling the lost pieces of myself home.

First I started playing it while I walked down the street. Then I began having a little dance party each night in my apartment. Then I would play it in my head before a big creative presentation or before I taught a Spirited Session. Eventually I conjured up the courage to share it with Craig and now he sings it to me!

WORK YOUR LIGHT

Choose your own theme song. It can be any song in the entire world. Or if you feel the urge, create one yourself. Put it on your iPod, iTunes, or Spotify and listen to it daily.

△

WRITE YOUR OWN TAG LINE

If you had a legacy what would it be? The simple act of condensing yourself down into a tag line forces us to really get clear on what it is we most want to share with the world. It doesn't need to be world changing.

The tag line acts as a manifesto of who you are and what you stand for. It might sound silly, but the clarity that comes from having your own personal tag line is a Godsend when you're faced with a tricky decision. You can weigh up each option and see which fits your tag line. It's also a great measure for checking if your life is aligned.

My friend Blair Milan had his own tag line: 'Good Times.' Not someone who suffered from confidence issues, Blair used his tag line any chance he got. When signing off emails, when saying cheers, when someone was describing something that happened to them, when he was relaying a story. You name it he'd drop it in there.

Arriving in Sydney after his death we went straight into funeral organizational mode. The theme of the wake was 'Good Times' and it was the biggest extravaganza that The Sydney Theatre Company had ever seen: singing, comedy, speeches, videos, and montages of all things Blair. (*He would have adored the attention.*) There was even a 'Good Times Bar' as you walked in.

Blair lived his life so wholeheartedly in line with this manifesto that every single person knew what Blair had taught them about life. We got 'Good Times' badges made and everyone still wears them as a tribute to the way he lived his life.

Blair's whole life was a devotion to living, noticing, grabbing, and appreciating the 'Good Times' that life has to offer us all. People who barely even knew Blair were touched by the exuberant essence of his spirit. Because he was so clear on who he was and how he wanted to spread his light.

You are a rare gift. You have the ability to devote your life to whatever you wish. So what do you want your legacy to be? If you had to write one, what would your tag line be?

WORK YOUR LIGHT

My personal tag line is:

What in your life is not in alignment with your tag line?

△

COME OUT OF THE SPIRITUAL CLOSET

'Come out, come out wherever you are.'
GLINDA THE GOOD WITCH, *THE WIZARD OF OZ*

Come out of the spiritual closet, it's much better out here. With every day, it's becoming more and more socially acceptable to be openly 'spiritual.' But when you've been in the spiritual closet for some time, it can be pretty scary to reveal – particularly to the people who 'know you' best – that, actually, there's more to you than you've let them see.

I hid in my spiritual closet for over a decade. I would suss out people before I revealed just how 'spiritual' I really was with a whisper. But when my soul called me to align my life, I knew I needed to get naked. So little by little, I came out of the closet and timidly began to strip.

The biggest step was bringing my 'spiritual self' to my work. I started telling colleagues about weekend courses I was doing and leaving books I was reading on my desk (rather than hidden in my bag, so no one would see the covers). I shared my beliefs about the connection between creativity, spirituality, and ideas, which are waiting to be born. I then began dropping the 'S word' (spirit) in meetings, creating the phrase, 'Let your spirit be your brand.'

The more layers I shed, the more liberated I felt. The more of my authentic self I revealed, the more effortless work became because I was able to show up completely as me. Instead of fitting into a mold, I let myself overspill and expand. And then the overspilling bits became my 'thing.' I got pay rises, won awards, got promotions. The parts of me that I was trying to keep under control were the bits that everyone actually valued most. Getting naked was the most liberating and rewarding experience of my life.

We make the biggest impact in the world by sharing our full self. Are you bringing your full self to all areas of your life? The thing about getting naked is that you don't have to rip off your clothes all at once, so you're suddenly exposed in broad daylight for everyone to see and point. That's what nightmares are made of. The best stripteases leave you wanting more!

You might start by taking off your hat, then your scarf, and your gloves. Next might come your coat, followed by your heels. Eventually off comes your dress, bra, and the rest. The more layers that fall to the ground, the more people want to see.

The more of yourself you reveal, the easier it is for 'your people' to find you. It's much harder to spot someone when they are in a disguise.

WORK YOUR LIGHT

Are you in a spiritual closet? How can you start getting naked and align all areas of your life?

△

ALIGN YOUR LIFE

In order to thrive in a big way in (*we are all meant to thrive*), we must align our lives, so that all pieces flow in vibrational harmony. When we are in alignment everything in our life flows. When we are out of alignment, there's a feeling that something isn't quite right. If you understand the Law of Attraction you will know that in order to create what you desire, you must become an authentic vibrational match with what you want to attract. Just like a radio that is set to the wrong frequency, it is impossible to pick up the latest indie tunes when you are set to some boring talkback show.

Someone who is in complete alignment has aligned their energy, thoughts, actions, and words to be a vibrational match with what they want to attract. That is, it's not about longing to be something 'one day,' rather bringing your thoughts, actions, energy, and words into complete harmony so that you 'already are' all you are wishing to attract. If we manage to do this, it is impossible not to call in everything that you want. The catch, however, is being committed to make conscious daily actions that will bring you into alignment with that thing.

Just as I described in 'Show up and shine,' (see page 166), it wasn't until I was a 100 percent vibrational match with Hay House that I got the call. It took a while, but little by little – as my thoughts, words, energy, and actions came together into 100 per cent complete alignment – I became a vibrational match.

First was taking the leap from my career to throwing myself full-time into my intuitive coaching business, which I had been trained for, but never felt quite ready to start. Next was writing a little bit every day and putting together a book proposal. At this stage, I was given two opportunities to submit my proposal, but then it's no surprise that I didn't hear anything (because I still wasn't a vibrational match). A little disheartened, I scooped up my ego and committed to show up and write every day (just as I would if I was an author). Then came changing my thoughts around seeking approval from an external force before I felt legit, ready and deserving.

Finally, and most importantly, I found myself in a state of joy as I began to write for the love of it, rather than being attached to an outcome of being published. It became about answering the call for the joy of it rather than the end goal.

I lost myself in what lit me up, what happened, and the result of it was actually none of my business. Month by month, my thoughts, words, energy, and actions slowly but surely shifted into complete alignment with Hay House. On one hand, I worked extremely hard for a very long time (17 years, you could say) to get to that state of vibrational match, but the moment I was a complete vibrational match, it came without any effort, in an instant!

WORK YOUR LIGHT

What are you trying to call into or create in your life?

Are your thoughts, words, energy, and actions
in complete alignment with it?

Are you the same person in all areas of your life? (For
example, at work, at home, with friends, with strangers.)

△

BE A YES

Be a yes. A full-blown, 100 percent, hands down, hell yeah we're doing this no matter what kinda YES.

The Universe does not dabble in 'maybe' or 'kind of' or 'yeah, but.' It's either an unwavering 100 percent or not at all.

When we hold an intention, every single thing in the Universe either resonates or 'disonates' with that. If something resonates it is a 100 percent yes and it's going to come straight at you like a magnet or a seagull after your chips at the beach. If it's not quite 100 percent, the manifestation is going to be not quite 100 percent.

Every second of every day you are vibrating your 'yes,' 'no,' and 'maybe' thoughts and actions.

The clearer you can get on what makes you say 'HELL YEAH' and what makes you say 'HELL NO,' the more YESSES will come flying straight for you, landing right on your lap.

WORK YOUR LIGHT

How can you be more of a HELL YEAH for the things you are calling into your life (which are also the things that are calling you)?

△

TWITTER BIOS AND FITTING IN

We live in an age where we are called to define who we are in 140 characters. The amount of time I've spent editing my Twitter profile description should be a jail-able offence. Everyone I know has no idea how to describe what they 'do' and who they 'are' in a sentence.

That's because defining who you are in 140 characters is impossible! And more than that, you are a work in progress, an ever-evolving work of art so 140 characters will never sum you up. Ever! And that is a good thing.

Chances are you've probably had more than 140 lives (that's a lot of soul history and soul gifts packed into one vessel)... how could you possibly fit all that you are into 140 characters?

So if you can't find the words, it's probably not necessarily due to not knowing who you are. Maybe it's because you know you are all that and more.

Let your vibration do the talking for you.

△

VIBRATION IS THE BEST MARKETING TOOL

Your vibration is more powerful than your words could ever be. More powerful than what you wear, say, or do. More powerful than the best marketing strategy, publicist, and PR darling all put together.

Like attracts like.

It doesn't matter how 'in tune' someone is, they will pick up your vibration a mile off and make a split decision or judgment about you without even thinking about it.

Vibration has nothing to do with thought; it has everything to do with feeling. People make a decision about you based on these feelings, and they don't need to be 'in tune' to do it. We may not be able to put it in words but we can spot if someone is authentic in a nanosecond, because their energy matches their words.

The best web, copy, and advertising campaign is worthless if it doesn't match the brand's vibrational truth. If your words say one thing and your energy another, people just won't buy it, either figuratively or literally.

Energy doesn't lie.

The best test to see if your words match your vibration is to say them out loud. If they make you feel strong and true, then it is a match. If they make you squirm and cringe then it's not an authentic representation of what you are saying.

Your body can also give you clues. When you say something out loud, notice where you feel it in your body when you say something that is true versus when you say something that is not.

DO IT IN
A WAY THAT
ONLY YOU CAN.

△

YOU© – YOUR AUTHENTIC VOICE

If you feel drawn to share your message by writing, finding your authentic tone of voice is an important part of the process.

My first job in advertising was as a copywriter. I then went on to become a creative director where I directed teams of writers in finding the authentic tone of voice for loads of big brands. Finding your authentic tone of voice can take time, but here are some tools to help you express yours.

Be You©

You cannot find your authentic voice unless you know who you are. Knowing who you are takes time. Looking at what other people are doing, in an effort to do the same, won't work. It will water down your voice and won't be in alignment with who you are. Write as you speak. Write as you feel. If you are optimistic, be optimistic. If you are passionate, be passionate. If you are a hippy who has a dark sense of humor and loves pandas, be a hippy with a dark side that loves pandas. Be You©.

Write from your soul

Don't write what you think you should write; write what your soul is calling you to share. When I am writing from my soul my writing is extremely different to when I am writing from my head: the words come flowing and have a deeper, RICHER feel to them; my pace changes; and it feels passionate and free. Sometimes I write something and then read it back and think, 'Wow, that's beautiful,' because my head could not have possibly put it quite like that, no matter how hard it tried. I know then that the writing has come through me. It's not of me. When I write from my head it takes a lot more effort and doesn't have the same authenticity to it. It feels considered and rigid. No one wants to read that! Before you sit down to write, put your hand on your heart, take a breath, and listen to what your soul has to share.

Start talking

The only way to find your voice is to start talking (and being willing to get it wrong!). When I directed teams of writers I would review at least 20 headlines to find *the* one. Finding your voice is a process, we are multifaceted beings and so there are different directions we can take our writing. You need to be willing to get it wrong in order to know when you've got it right. Getting it wrong is just as important as getting it right.

Write to yourself

If you don't know what to say, write what you most need to hear. Your tribe resonates with you because they are aligned with your message. More likely than not, the messages your soul has for you will strike a chord in them too. You don't need to overcomplicate it. Read the chapter 'Letters to self' (see page 260) for more information on how to do this.

Be willing to get it wrong

You can't find your authentic voice without getting it wrong. Be willing to try things, to find your flow. You will know when you have tapped into your authentic tone because it will resonate with you. You might feel warmth in your heart, an all-over feeling of expansion or lightness. If it isn't aligned with who you are you might feel a burning in your belly.

Share don't compare

Don't compare yourself to someone else who has been writing for years. Don't rush it. Stay true. Be you. Sometimes ideas and phrases that are meant to be born will come through different writers – which is a tricky thing to tackle when you've spent a lot of time creating it. If someone else's stuff is similar to yours, check in with yourself to ensure that what you created came from an authentic place (and not from being on their social media feed). Do your best to make it your own and ask your soul for guidance.

Don't write for likes

Don't get disheartened if no one 'likes' or praises your writing. You have no idea how many hearts it has actually touched. Just show up and trust that if you have a message to share, the people who need to hear it most will see it.

Sharing vs. selling

Don't write to sell, write to share. If you're sharing on Facebook, your message will be competing with people's best friends in their newsfeed. Share what will provide value to your readers, not you.

I read something a while back (on Facebook but can't remember who posted it!) that stuck with me, which went something like this:

'I don't share to teach or convince others, I share to make those who feel the same as me feel less alone.'

I adore this.

That's why we share our story, our message, and our soul.

A *freakin'* men.

△

YOU© – YOUR AUTHENTIC VISUAL STYLE

Part of shining your light is expressing your light in a way that is in visual alignment with who you are.

The way to shine your light the furthest is to do things in a way that is completely authentic to you, and a great way to explore your look and feel is to pin. I get everyone who does a 'Work Your Light Mentorship' or online course with me to start a personal brand pin board over at www.pinterest.com. You can keep it public or make it private. You could even name it, e.g. Amy©.

There are no rules to what you pin, but you might find the following guidance helpful in getting you started.

Pin what makes your heart expand
Don't analyze why you are pinning, just pin the things that make your heart expand. Pin what is a YES and scroll past what is a NO.

Find your own style
You want your brand to be a unique expression of you, not a second-rate version of someone else. Don't insult your authenticity by 'borrowing' someone else's look and feel. Draw your inspiration from your inner compass. These things take time so let it evolve. Let your inner light lead the way.

Don't feel guilty
If you have any feelings of 'this is a waste of time,' or 'I should be doing things that are more important,' shake those bad boys off.

Look for directions

After a little while (it might be a month or a couple of weeks), look at your board as a whole. You will begin to notice a couple of different directions starting to come through. Certain types of colors, photography styles, and typography will start bubbling up and a certain attitude will start to shine through. All of these things are priceless when it comes to finding your own authentic visual expression. Delete the things that don't resonate as much and keep the ones that do. What you want to get to is a consistent over-arching unique visual style that represents you.

Working with designers

If, at some stage, you plan to work with a designer to create a website, having a brand board is imperative. There are *so* many websites out there that look the same. One of the reasons this happens is not enough thought going into getting really clear on the unique brand, and so the creative direction the designer gets is 'make it like [*insert site name*] and [*insert site name*].'

Briefing a designer is really tricky because people respond subjectively to visuals. And as a designer, being briefed by someone who doesn't know what they are looking for is like designing in the dark. It is IMPOSSIBLE to describe visuals objectively.

I've worked with many designers and can't stress the importance of establishing a clear and unique visual direction before you jump into creating your site. For the cover of this book, I spent two days coming up with mood boards for all of the possible visual directions to brief the designer.

If you've done the groundwork on who you are and what type of visuals resonate with you, then you'll be well on your way to shining your light in a visually authentic way.

You are a work in progress

Be open to evolving your look and feel as you evolve as a person. Your style should always be anchored in who you are; however, as you grow, your design should too. THIS is what makes it impossible to mimic.

WORK YOUR LIGHT

If you don't have a Pinterest account already, sign up and start pinning. I'd recommend around 10 minutes a day for a period of a month to start seeing a nice visual style coming through. If you want extra guidance on developing your unique brand, I offer mentoring and online courses that will help you shine your light in a super authentic way.

△

IT'S NOT ABOUT YOU

Living a life of service means showing up and shining our light regardless of what people think. If you dim your light because you feel inadequate, you are doing the world a disservice. The moment you bring your drama, fear or self-image into the picture you make it about you. It's not about you.

Recently I learned this one in a big way. I'm part of a Six Sensory Mastermind Skype support group of six intuitives from around the world. On a recent call one of them said, 'Rebecca has been a bit quiet today – so Rebecca, what's up?' (*Sometimes it's annoying having intuitives as friends!*). I told them that I was feeling nervous about a big speaking event I had coming up.

I told them, 'I know it's silly but I am feeling really nervous and am doubting myself because all the other speakers are much more experienced.'

Monika then firmly but lovingly replied, 'It sounds like that's Rebecca's ego talking. It's afraid of how she will be received. When really it's none of her business. She needs to trust that whoever booked her trusts that what she has to offer is exactly what the attendees need to hear. She needs to get out of the way and stop making it about her.'

Everyone agreed. Including me.

My ego was getting in the way; letting my fear of not being good enough prevent me from showing up and serving to the best of my ability. I was spending valuable time, which I could use to prepare, worrying. And had I gone on stage in a fear state then I wouldn't have been giving them the best, most present me. I heard the message loud and clear:

It's so not about me!

When I started giving intuitive readings and coaching, I used to do the same thing. I'd look to my clients for validation that I 'got it right,' that the information I was receiving resonated and was helpful. Now, I know that my job is more about holding space and being as present as I possibly can. I trust that I am the vehicle for the Universe to work through. And whatever words I have to share are exactly the ones they need to hear.

How people receive you is none of your business. You were given a unique set of gifts, life experiences, and passions. Your only job is to share them. Whatever experience you are facing right now

You are ready for it!

You would not have been given it, if you weren't. You do deserve to be here. Regardless of how nervous or unprepared you feel, suck it up and shine your light anyway. The world needs your light.

It doesn't mean that doubt doesn't exist. Doubt and fear are normal parts of being human. Admit your fears. My teachers taught me that if I am scared of something the best cure is saying it out loud; it makes it a little less scary.

WORK YOUR LIGHT

How is your fear getting in the way of you
stepping into your biggest self?

△

YOU ARE NOT FOR EVERYONE

The world is filled with people who, no matter what you do, will point blank not like you. But it is also filled with those who will love you fiercely. They are your people. You are not for everyone and that's OK. Talk to the people who can hear you.

Don't waste your precious time and gifts trying to convince them of your value, they won't ever want what you're selling. Don't convince them to walk alongside you. You'll be wasting both your time and theirs and will likely inflict unnecessary wounds, which will take precious time to heal. You are not for them and they are not for you; politely wave them on, and continue along your way. Sharing your path with someone is a sacred gift; don't cheapen this gift by rolling yours in the wrong direction.

Keep facing your true north.

△

BE OK WITH WHERE YOU ARE

Be OK with where you are and all that you are right now – especially the bits that you are working on. The people you are here to guide are the ones who are a few steps behind you. You don't need to have it all sorted, or be an expert...

It's your humanness that truly touches people, not your superhuman-ness.

When we first embark on our journey of spiritual awakening, we can find ourselves thinking that we 'get it' – as if there is a finite destination to arrive at. When the opposite is actually true. The more we know, the less we actually know.

You don't need to pretend or prove that you have it together, rather, just share what you have figured out so far. We are all in this school of life together. There is no final destination, no end point, just increased consciousness and a deeper understanding.

Every moment is an opportunity to deepen our learning about life and ourselves. When we resist saying, 'Oh this, I already know this,' we open the door for life to come in and touch our soul even more deeply than before.

We are all eternal students. I am so happy to have learned this recently, even more deeply than I knew it before. And I'm looking forward to learning it even more deeply than I think I know it now. Sometimes words get in the way of truth.

Soften your mind, and your soul will be touched.

$\triangle$

CREATIVITY AND BEING
A CLEAR CHANNEL

When you tap into the flow of Source energy you are a clear channel for creations to flow through you. When you allow Source to flow through you, a beautiful thing happens – just like sunbeams shining through a stained-glass window: the light passes through your authentic self and creates something that no one else could have created.

Many of my clients fear that what they have to say isn't valid because:

1.   It has already been said by someone else (who beat them to it and is already established);

2.   Or, lots of other people have been through a similar experience, so what's so special about them?

As we allow the light to flow through the stained-glass windows of our soul, our vibration that the creation holds draws people in.

If there are people who have been through, or are going through, similar experiences as you, then all the more urgency for you to share your message and creations now. If you have heard the call (and I believe we all have) start creating now. Don't waste your time looking over your shoulder, do it in a way that only you can.

WORK YOUR LIGHT

What is stopping you from expressing your
message or creations more courageously?

△

INVOKING YOUR MUSE

Everyone on the planet has the ability to be creative and birth ideas. Creativity flows through us and while we might be there when the creation happens, there is a mysterious force that delivers it. This book has been written this way and many writers and artists admit to birthing their creations the same way. I call this creative force 'the muse.'

The muse is always on the lookout for people to receive creations that are waiting to be born. But if we don't show up every day, or only when we feel like it, the muse will move onto someone else. She's promiscuous like that. It's not personal. It's just the way of the muse.

The muse wants us to act on our ideas without delay. We are the vehicles for the creation to come into the world. Pretty much every time I have stalled on a big idea or acted a little slowly, someone else has come up with a similar phrase, creation, or idea in unison. When your muse speaks, act.

The more we show up every day to connect with our muse, the clearer the communication gets and the more effortlessly the creations start flowing.

When a muse chooses you, they choose you because you are the perfect vehicle for their message. It's that YOU-NESS they want, your unique creative fingerprint. A perfect concoction of life experience, upbringing, city, body type, and voice.

WORK YOUR LIGHT

What creations or ideas are waiting to be born by you?

△

LETTERS TO SELF

'A bird doesn't sing because it has the answers,
it sings because it has a song.'
Maya Angelou

When embarking on writing this book, my teacher Sonia told me to 'write to your most interested reader... you.' I had heard this from her years earlier when she described the process of writing her first book, where her friend Julia Cameron had asked her to think of it as writing a letter every day. But to be honest I didn't know what she meant. Then it dawned on me, it's not because I'm my most interested reader (because I just love reading my own words), it's because at some point in my life these were the words I most needed to hear. Eureka!

Every day when I sit down to write, that is exactly what I do. It doesn't matter if it's a new chapter, a Facebook update, a tweet, a blog post, or scribbles in my notebook. I allow my fingers to be taken over by the energy of what my heart most needs to hear. It could be what it most needs to hear today, or it could be what I most needed to hear at a different moment of my life, a moment when I most needed to be shown the way, to be reassured, to be encouraged.

We are all linked through the most magnificent web of golden threads. What your heart needs to hear is what another does too.

If you are sharing your writing, don't write to teach or convince, write to soften your own heart. Allow each word that comes through you to be medicine for your soul. The people who need to hear it will be drawn by your words, by your message, by your truth, by your song. When you allow the wiser you to write to yourself, you allow your head to get out of the way and your wise higher self to take over.

Write to heal yourself. For as we heal ourselves, we can't help but heal the world at large.

WORK YOUR LIGHT

Write your own 'Letter to Self.' Get a blank piece of paper and write at the top, 'Dear [*insert your name*].'

Fill the page with the words you most need to hear. Maybe they're the words you most need to hear today, or maybe they're the words you most needed to hear five, 10, even 20 years ago. Without judgment let them come flowing.

If you feel inspired by what you have written, you might want to share your words on Facebook, in a blog, or wherever feels right.

We are all in this shared experience called life together. What is healing for you will likely be healing for someone else too. Serve the world by being you.

△

YOUR SOUL'S VOICE

'The planet needs your soul's unique tone to harmonise.'
SERA BEAK

We each hold a truth deep within us that longs to be expressed. Sculpted for lifetimes, the voice of your soul is like no other. It carries with it wisdom that can only be gained through soul growth. Through remembering, tapping into, and expressing this unique tone, we not only heal ourselves, we also heal the planet. Indeed, the world needs harmonizing drastically.

Our soul's voice is slightly different to the voice we are used to speaking with, and it can take a lot of courage to find and share it with the world.

My soul's voice comes through the most strongly when I write. It is deep and wise, it is compassionate and motherly, it is courageous and knowing, it is petrified and fierce. It is the result of lifetimes of speaking out and being silenced, of devastating grief and absolute devotion.

I know when I am writing from my soul as my whole energy changes, my writing style shifts slightly and it feels like I am being pulled by a gentle current in a deep, warm, ocean.

As we shed the layers of our personality and start letting our soul speak through us, we discover that we actually have a very clear message that longs to be shared. The more we speak it, the clearer it gets. However, more often than not, the message our soul truly longs to express can take extreme courage to share.

While I knew from an early age that my calling was to write, teach, and speak, I was petrified by the idea. I knew my soul had wisdom to share, but I kept making excuses for why I wasn't ready to step forward. When I was young, I rationalized that I didn't have any life experience to teach; once I had those extreme experiences I argued that I needed yet another modality to learn before I would feel 'ready.' I'd watch other people walking the path, knowing that it was similar to the one set out ahead of me, but I was paralyzed by an extreme fear that I just couldn't shake. It wasn't like normal fear, I felt as though if I spoke my truth I would risk my life.

One day, before attending a weekend workshop, I prayed to the Universe to help me release this fear for real. Sure enough, on the first day my teacher Sonia asked me to come to the front of the class to work on letting go of old energetic patterns from past lives. Held by the class, I journeyed from lifetime to lifetime where I was betrayed and killed for speaking my truth. A scholar in Ancient Greece, a witch in the Middle Ages, an Essene in the time of Jesus Christ, a priest in France, a mystic in Ancient Egypt.

Lifetime upon lifetime came flooding back and my soul showed me why I felt so much pain about speaking out and stepping forward. As Sonia and Shamanic healer Debra Grace guided me, I allowed myself to remember all of the pain and to release it through my tears and voice. I sobbed more than I ever had and surrendered the grief, anger, betrayal, and pain to the light.

Through tapping into this extreme grief, I was able to understand why I felt such extreme fear over stepping forward. Now when I feel the fear to speak out I remember all of these courageous men and women who my soul has embodied and I feel them standing alongside me. I see how all of these lives have led to the one I am living now, and how lucky I am to be living at a time in history in which it is easier to stand up than it ever has been before.

While my soul remembers the past pain, I choose to be strengthened by it. I allow these experiences to come through in my writing and I thank all of these amazing men and women for rising and rising. If you are having trouble stepping forward and sharing your soul's truth, it is likely that you have soul memory of being rejected in the past for doing just that.

There has never been a better time in history than right now to rise up and speak your truth. It is not only needed, it is necessary. If you feel fearful of speaking up and stepping out, know that you are not alone and, as Sera Beak so beautifully puts it, 'the world needs your unique tone in order to harmonize.' As we each rise up, we make it easier for the next to do the same.

WORK YOUR LIGHT

What fear do you have that is stopping you sharing your voice?

What is behind this fear?

How is your soul voice different to your normal speaking voice?

△

SPEAK UP, I CAN'T HEAR YOU

Speak up. I can't hear you.

I want to know how similar we are and that I am not actually alone.

Speak up. I can't hear you.

I want to be touched by your voice and raised up by your vibe.

Speak up. I can't hear you.

I want to hear how you struggled and how
after it all you still managed to rise.

Speak up. I can't hear you.

I want to be inspired by your journey and reminded
that, perhaps, one day soon I too can shine.

Speak up. I can't hear you.

△

RAISE THEM UP, DON'T CUT THEM DOWN

'Comparison is an act of violence against the self.'
IYANLA VANZANT

Raise them up, not cut them down.

The sign of true success is someone who enjoys raising up those around them. Let's all rise up together; let's encourage, not compete.

When one woman shines her light, she makes the path brighter for the next one to come. There are enough people asleep for us all to awaken with our light. Next time someone is rising, shine your light on them.

You'll shine all the more brightly for it.

WORK YOUR LIGHT

Who in your life do you feel competitive with?

What's behind the competitiveness?

△

IF YOU'RE COMPETING WITH SOMEONE...

That woman you're jealous of, envious, who has what you want.

They are you and you are them. And you're both doing your best.

That girl you're competing with, who presses your buttons, who doesn't deserve it as much as you.

They are you and you are them. And you're both doing your best.

That chick that annoys you, who beat you to it, who is doing what you were planning on doing and now it's too late.

They are you and you are them. And you're both doing your best

That lady who somehow got lucky and just landed on her feet.

They are you and you are them. And you're both doing your best.

That sister who courageously followed her calling, and is now bravely shining her light.

They are you and you are them. And you're both doing your best.

If you pay enough attention when you look in her eyes, you'll see your light reflected back.

For they are you and you are them. And you're both just doing your best.

MANTRA

I choose not to compare myself to others. I show
up and let the Universe work through me, knowing
that what I have to offer is enough.

BE AN ENCOURAGER

Be an encourager, not a discourager.

The one who wants the best for others and celebrates when they win.

Be an encourager, not a discourager.

The one who sees the light in those around them
and reminds them of it when they fall.

Be an encourager, not a discourager.

The one who acknowledges their jealous thoughts,
but chooses to replace them with others.

Be an encourager, not a discourager.

The one who admits when they are down but doesn't
demand that they take others with them.

Be an encourager, not a discourager.

The one who remembers that we are actually all on the same team.

△

THERE'S ROOM ENOUGH FOR EVERYONE

There is enough room for everyone. Your special unique bag of gifts, stories, struggles, triumphs, energy, and tools is like no one else's. The way you look, the city you're from, your voice, your body size, your smile... embrace it, don't change it. There is enough room for everyone.

In this social age, it's easy to see those who are walking a similar path as your competition. Don't let your ego see that person as separate, we're actually all on the same team, there's no need to compete.

There is enough room for everyone.

YOUR SOUL'S GOT THINGS TO SAY.

DEMYSTIFYING THE MYSTIC

The Ancient Egyptians believed that we have 360 senses all linked to the organs of our body (which coincides with the chakras, see page 193). While we may be more technologically advanced than the ancients, we are not as awake as they were.

Our wise sixth sense is not just reserved for the mystics and the psychics, it is available to us all. We just need to look within. The mystics knew this. But the sharing of this knowledge was not exactly convenient for those who were trying to control the masses.

As we move out of the shadow of the patriarchal system (where power and control reign supreme), light is being shed on this female archetype that is an embodiment of the Divine Feminine. I am she. You are she. We are all her. She was our grandmother's grandmother, our grandmother's grandmother's grandmother. She is all of the women who refused to stop rising up. And all of the men too.

If we all woke up to our intuitive nature, inner power, and authentic magic, the world would be a very different place. It's happening, slowly but surely, and you're at the forefront.

As more and more of us rise up to our inner wisdom and true authentic power, we embrace the authentic magic that dwells within. An era where it is safe for us all to shine as big and bright as humanly possible. An era where there is enough room for us all to follow our soul's callings and express our gifts freely. An era where we are all awake and living consciously.

My wish is that we all find the courage to lead the way. That we continue to rise up regardless of people who think that we are 'too much.' Now is the time we have been rising for. For centuries, for this moment.

**The Divine Feminine is within all of us
and she is ready to rise up.**

Δ

THE MYSTIC ALWAYS RISES

As she let her soul sing to her, she let go of lifetimes' worth of silenced truth missiles cemented in the deepest caverns of her soul. A voice snuffed out for centuries, for saying too much, for standing up too much, for being too much.

Her intuition and bigness restrained for centuries, but not any more. She could not be locked away, muted, or extinguished any longer. Not now. Not ever again.

As she let her spirit move her, she danced right through the flames. Resentment, anger, and memories stomped out with every blazing convulsion, sway, and kick. Sensing her in the distance, one by one her sisters joined her, knowing this dance by heart.

The movement created space for their tears, which flowed deeper than all of the rivers and lakes from all of the ages. Soothing and cooling the burning that once enveloped her entire being. Her whole body. All of her bodies. All of their bodies. All of our bodies.

Never forgetting. But still rising, just as she planned to. Just as we planned to. Rising and rising and rising and rising and rising. Standing taller than all the sisters who came before and will continue to come again.

The mystic always rises.

△

YOUR HEART IS ELASTIC

Your heart is elastic. It can grow or expand according to how much you are ready to receive. It can be stretched and filled up with all of the unlimited love and support that is flowing through the Universe.

If you've experienced real depths in your life, you'll know that just when you thought things couldn't get any worse, they sometimes do. The same goes for the good stuff too, though. The only limit to how much good you can receive is your perception of how much good you can receive. Your heart is elastic and your capacity for joy is as much as you say it is. Which is a lot. In fact, it's unlimited. So, how much good can you handle?

MANTRA

Every moment of every day, I am expecting
and welcoming good things.

LET THE UNIVERSE SUPPORT YOU

The Universe is here to support you as much as you let it.

Many of my Lightworker clients have a block around earning proper abundance for their soul work, particularly the healers (you don't need to be a healer to be a Lightworker). As if it is not quite fair to receive real prosperity for giving love, shining your light and being of service. I disagree.

Devoting your life to something bigger is not a small feat. There are many things you need in order to do your work; you deserve to be supported as you do it. Right now for me, I am spending most of my time writing and working with clients through giving Akashic record readings and mentoring.

In order for me to be of service for my clients I need to eat well, meditate, rest, and keep investing in my learning. If I have more than four clients a day my energy gets depleted (working in the subtle realms can be pretty tiring). I'm not soft or afraid of hard work (if anything I overwork), but I have found that I cannot be of service unless I listen to my body.

The work that you are called to do is priceless. As such, the people who choose to answer their highest calling and be of service should be bountifully supported. And you will be, if you allow it.

MANTRA

I let go of the outcome and I allow myself to be supported
by the Universe in ways that I could not even imagine.

△

EXPANSION AND NEVER-ENDING GROWTH

'What is the difference
Between your experience of Existence
And that of a saint?
The saint knows
That the spiritual path is a sublime chess game with God
And that the Beloved
Has just made such a Fantastic Move
That the saint is now continually
Tripping over Joy
And bursting out in Laughter
And saying, "I Surrender!"
Whereas, my dear, I am afraid you still think
You have a thousand serious moves.'

TRIPPING OVER JOY, HAFIZ

We are all in this Earth school of life together; the learning never stops. Have you ever noticed how just after you have a spiritual breakthrough, the Universe sends something your way and it feels like you're at the beginning again?

It's so frustrating because our mind is so linear and likes to think that we are getting somewhere in particular – a definite end point or destination. But what I have come to realize is that really we are just deepening our learning, understanding, and remembering. We are all students and there's always more deepening to experience.

When we say to the Universe, 'Please use me,' or 'Let me be of service to the world,' it's as if the Universe cries, 'Hooray!' and then commits to sending things our way to make us better equipped to be of service.

These things, experiences, or people, then do their best to mirror back to us the part of our shadow that could do with a bit of work. Shining a light on all the things that you're facing that will make you even better equipped to serve in the highest capacity. If there are any healers or coaches out there you'll know what I am saying. I've had my most powerful sessions with clients who are dealing with the exact thing that I was struggling with the day before.

There is no end destination to get to, no time to arrive. Rather, more of yourself to embrace and expand into.

One of my friends reminded me of a cool fact about saints. She said, 'Why do you think that most saints are not deemed saints until after they have died? It's because all the people who were around to vouch for their humanness have passed away.'

I love that so much.

On our journey towards 'enlightenment' it's important to remember that we are human, and with being human comes having an ego. No matter how masterful we are, we are all students and the learning never ends. And that's a good thing. But as we begin to accept our challenging experiences as opportunities for growth, what would have previously felt like a tsunami crashing through our life can be reframed to be an opportunity to expand. Which is why we are here in the first place.

The amazing thing about this time we are living in is that there is a mass-awakening happening. In the past when people 'woke up' many would withdraw from society and go sit in a cave. But now, I believe that we are being called to integrate our awakened consciousness in all parts of society. With every new person who wakes up, the vibration of the planet also increases. With every conscious decision we each make (whether it's to meditate, follow a career that is calling us or going veggie) we add to the raised consciousness of the planet.

There is no right or wrong way to expand and grow, just many different paths.

Your inner guidance system knows what's the right one for you, don't let anyone tell you different.

△

IT'S TIME TO STEP UP

The planet is beckoning. Coaxing. Calling you. To step into your wholeness. To step up and into all of you. The big you. The complete you. The one that's full of light. She's already in you. Give in to the stirring. Give in to the niggle. Answer the calling. You are the message. The time has come. You are needed here. Let's get to work.

△

YOU WEREN'T BORN FOR THE SIDELINES

You were not born for the sidelines, for the nose bleeders or the wings.

Raise the curtain, take the microphone, there's a song for you to sing.

You were born with a message; you have
something important to share.

Instead of resisting your soul's yearnings, make
your life one big moving prayer.

Stop waiting for permission, don't pretend to be blind.

Don't compare yourself to others; you are one of a very unique kind.

Your spot at the table is waiting; your seat has already been assigned.

Now take a breath, a good old leap and get ready to shine.

Come out from the sidelines, from the nose bleeders and the wings.

Raise the curtain, take the stage, it's your soul's song you need to sing.

LIGHT UP THE WAY.

△

YOU GO FIRST

You go first. It's time, you're ready, your soul is calling for you to lead the way.

If you can't quite find the courage to do it for you, then do it for:

Emma Ball, Ollie Neveu, Melanie Mackie, and Sanja Plavljanic-Sirola. Do it for Marlene Gourlay, Kirsty Hobbs, Jennifer Mole, and Bianca Young. Do it for Joanne Williams, Rosemarie St Louis, Bianca Filoteo, and Anne-Marie Tiller. Do it for Roz Grimble, Jen Bollands, Zoe Brewer, and Meghan Genge. Do it for Kay Blanchard, Brooke Steff, Vicky Maxwell, and Jane Wright. Do it for Natasha Van Staden, Michelle Van Caneghem, Alexis Williams, and Laura Paterson. Do it for Naomi Baird, Jessica Noyes, Narinder Bassan, and Emily Johnston. Do it for Libby Horsman, Bethany Love, Sheila Ann Lacey, and Suzan Ward. Do it for Victoria Cottle, Claire Ashman, Amelia Pearson, and Lizzie Houlbrooke. Do it for Kimberley Jones, Susannah Lee, Cath Dreamcatcher, Melissa LaJoie, and Louise Nyakoojo. Do it for Sonia Kaur, Jacquelyn Hayley, Tric Wright, and Helen Thomas. Do it for Hayley Wintermantle, Carolyn Sykes, Heather Burke, and Monika Laschkolnig. Do it for Renee Vos de Wael, Natalie Sneddon, Caya Munro, and Ruthie Kolle Hayes. Do it for Jacqueline Hulan, Giallian Marks, Lisa Barner, and Cornelia Blom. Do it for Laura Martin, Lesa Cochrane, Danielle Mercurio, and Rachel Whitehead. Do it for Juliana Ilieva, Karen Anderton, Aoife Anastasia, and Carol Harley. Do it for Viv Ferrari, Susanne Snellman, Kristy Blaikie, and Frankie Stone. Do it for Kay Jackson, Jett Black, Sarah Hook, and Susan Young. Do it for Lucy Paltnoi, Bill Gee, Louise Androlia, and Emily Riggs. Do it for Georgina Davis, Tania Constantini-Zimmermann, Shelly Drew, and Oeda O'Hara. Do it for Bekky May, Sarah Wilder, Lisa Caddick, and Lucy Milan Davis. Do it for Rachel Savage, Yolande Diver, Vienda Maria, and Carly Jennings. Do it for Annabelle Catherine Chambers, Nicola Phipard-Shears, Lisa Rose, and Keyon Bayani. Do it for Jen Claire Harrison, Emma Pedersen, Nathalie Hollywood, and Nicolle Smith. Do it for Gina Corneille Lilasong, Lizzie Bengal, Helen Hodgson, and Ailish Lucas. Do it for Jo Kilma, Kathryn Davy, Sonja Lockyer, and Alex Beadon. Do it for Kindra Murphy, Graciela Vega, Lauren Raso, and Helene Reinbolt. Do it for Martha Brown, Diana Sophie Walles, and Christina Walsh. Do it for Roslyn Tebble, Shelly Cameron, Debbie Bolton, and Lucy Sheridan-Wightman. Do it for Bea Bea's Baker, Lisa Marie Pittman, Renee de Villeneuve, and Amanda Emmett. Do it for Belinda Kerruish, Madalyn DeMolet, Zoe Wells, and Tiana-Marie Jones. Do it for Lily Holliday, Pauline Kehoe, Cllaire Brady, and Amy Davidson. Do it for Loren Honey, Julia Davis, Anne-Marie Williams, and Cassie Raine. Do it for Kate Sawyer, Marrsha Troyer Massino, Lindsay Pera, and Jennifer Caine. Do it for Jojo Williams, Jenifer Mole, Jayne Goldheart, and Lisa Crowned Jewelz Davis. Do it for Fiona Pearson, Gillian Marks, Jacqueline Haley, and Claire Maria Atkins. Do it for Marisa Madeline Beatey, Emma Pechey, Fiona Radman, and Betsy Bass. Do it for Jennifer Cainssino, Lindsay Perawyer, Julia Davis, Clare Sophia Voyant, and Katie Gee. Do it for Sheila Dickson, Dana May, Amy Firth, and Jaqueline Kolek. Do it for Cath Dreamdancer Gearing, Adriana Zooma, Zoe Caldwell, and Peg Watt.

Do it for your best friend and your sister, your aunt and your mother.

Do it for all the women who came before and all that will ever be.

Do it for all of these women, and all the rest.

For when they watch you go first, they'll find the courage to go next.

△

LETTER TO A LIGHTWORKER II

This is the dawn of a new day and the day of a new dawn.

You have the power to spark global change just by being you.

Every decision you make creates a ripple in the
interconnected sea that joins all life; there is nothing
too big or too small, every conscious act counts.

Follow what lights you up and what makes you feel
expansive. Don't worry about what it is, what people will
think, or the way it should be done. Just lose yourself in the
doing and invite the Universe to work through you.

Go 'in' every day. Sit down with yourself and listen. Your Inner Guru
should be the only authority of your life. Ask it to light your way.

Your soul knows the fastest way home. Act
on its whispers, especially when it's telling you
something that you don't want to hear.

Trade in controlling and forcing for allowing and trusting. The
Universe is waiting to support you. But first you've got to leap.

Breathe through your fear or speak it out loud but, whatever you
do, don't hide it away. Have a cup of tea with it and see it for
what it really is... an invitation to expand. Accept the invitation.

To expand doesn't mean you must push your energy onto
someone else. Shining can happen from a quiet space too,
you don't need to be an extrovert to do it. The Universe is
expanding every second. No matter how much you grow,
there is always going to be more than enough room.

To 'be the light' doesn't take strenuous effort, but it does require you to show up. Show up now. And now. And now. And now. And now. And now. And now. And now. And now.

You're not normal, you're extraordinary. Your attempt to fit in will never work. You were not born to live in a box. Overspill. Expand. Take up space. Anything less will be a tragic waste.

Embrace the energy that wants to come through you. There are books waiting to be written, speeches waiting to be given, mountains waiting to be climbed, and babies waiting to be birthed. Raise your hand, take a great big leap, and enjoy the ride.

This is the dawn of a new day and the day of a new dawn.

Thank you for lighting the way.

△

THE ARMY OF LIGHT IS ALWAYS RECRUITING

The Army of Light wants you! You are being recruited to light up the world by being you. In return for shining your light in a way that only you can and listening to the callings of your soul, the Universe will support you wholly.

Warning: Your dreams may not play out as you think they will. There is a considerable chance they will work out better than you could possibly imagine.

Name: ....

Signature: ....

Name: THE UNIVERSE ....

Signature: *The Universe* ....

I'M NOT AFRAID.
I WAS BORN
TO DO THIS.

JOAN OF ARC

△

THANK YOU

Here we are, at the end of these pages, but perhaps at just the beginning of a longer journey together.

From the bottom of my heart I hope that these words have in some way served you in coming back home to the wisdom of your soul.

Sometimes words cannot express all that our heart feels, but I trust that anything missed your heart and soul will catch.

Your being here matters, your rising up matters, your expansion matters, your courageousness matters, your consciousness matters, shining your light matters. No act is too big or too small. Keep rising up.

Thank you for your presence, for showing up, and your light.

Thank you for serving the world by being you.

I am so glad you are here.

Only love,

Rebecca

△

ONE THING

If you could take only one thing from this book, this is what I would choose it to be: Your soul is always calling you in the direction of your wholeness, flow, dreams, and purpose (and everything else). But you have to show up to it to hear it.

Non-negotiable daily spiritual practice is the only way that I have found to do this. Show up to the callings of your soul and the Universe will open its arms to support you.

In short: Meditate every day.

And wait for the magic to happen.

△

BASK IN THE LIGHT SOME MORE

Get on the list

Add some light to your inbox by signing up to my email at www.rebeccacampbell.me/signup

Ladies of the Light

Connect with other like-hearted soul sisters at www.rebeccacampbell.me/ladiesofthelight

Instant Guidance Oracle

Get some guidance using my free Instant Guidance Oracle at www.rebeccacampbell.me/instant-guidance

Going deeper

If you dig this book and want to go deeper, check out my online courses and mentoring at www.rebeccacampbell.me

Connect

www.rebeccacampbell.me

www.facebook.com/rebeccathoughts

www.instagram.com/rebeccathoughts

www.twitter.com/rebeccathoughts

www.pinterest.com/campbellrebecca

Δ

I RECOMMEND

Books

The Artist's Way, Julia Cameron (Pan Books, 1995)

Ask and It Is Given, Abraham-Hicks (Hay House, 2008)

Boundless Love, Miranda Macpherson (Ebury Press, 2002)

Eat Pray Love, Elizabeth Gilbert (Bloomsbury, 2009)

I Remember Union, Flo Calhoun (All Worlds Pub, 1992)

The Lightworker's Way, Doreen Virtue (Hay House, 2005)

Reveal, Meggan Watterson (Hay House, 2013)

Tribes, Seth Godin (Piatkus, 2008)

Walking Home, Sonia Choquette (Hay House, 2014)

The War of Art, Steven Pressfield (Black Irish Entertainment LLC, 2012)

Wings of Forgiveness, Kyle Gray (Hay House, 2015)

Your Big Beautiful Book Plan, Danielle LaPorte and Linda Sivertsen

Music

Krishna Das: www.krishnadas.com

Chloë Goodchild: www.thenakedvoice.com

Baird Hersey: www.bairdhersey.com

Jai Jagdeesh: www.jai-jagdeesh.com

Light Is The New Black Playlist: www.lightisthenewblack.com

Gurunam Singh: www.gurunamsingh.com

Nikki Slade: www.freetheinnervoice.com

Events and courses

B School: http://marieforleobschool.com

Emerging Women: http://www.emergingwomen.com

Hay House Writer's Workshop: http://www.hayhouse.co.uk

School of the Modern Mystic: http://schoolofthemodernmystic.com

Six Sensory Living: http://www.soniachoquette.com

Spirit Junkie Masterclass: http://spiritjunkies.com

Spirited Sessions: http://www.thespiritedproject.com

△

ACKNOWLEDGMENTS

To my teacher and mentor, Sonia Choquette. For all of the teachings (even in my sleep!), for guiding the way through the crumbling of the past, for encouraging me to teach and write, and for handing this book to Michelle at Hay House.

To Craig Gourlay. For giving me the experience of rising in love, for riding the magic carpet, for your eight-ness, and for the limitless encouragement and support during the writing of these pages (and for putting up with my extreme messiness!).

To Trevor and Julie Campbell. For teaching me the importance of education, giving me every opportunity possible, supporting me every step of the way, and for giving me wings to fly on my own.

To Angela Wood. For your friendship, courage, huge heart, all of the D & M's, and for being such a huge catalyst in my awakening.

To Blair, Wildcat, and Adrian. For all of the good times, and for showing me how to truly live.

To Matt. For your unconditional encouragement, and for all of the growth made possible because of our relationship.

To Amy Firth. For your sisterhood and helping me edit my story in the best possible way. To Sheila Dickson for your friendship and being even more excited than me when great things happen.

To Chela Davidson for supporting me mid-leap. To Andrrea Hess for giving me insight into who I am at soul level and the work I am here to do. To Nikki Slade and Gail Larson for helping me free my soul's voice. To Miranda Macpherson for your powerful teachings and holding energy. To Gurunam Singh, Krishna Das, Baird Hersey, and Jai-Jagdeesh for your devotional music that touches my heart like no other.

To Jaqui Kolek, Louise Androlia, and my Six Sensory mastermind sisters (Betsy Bass, Monika Laschkolnig, Susanne Snellman, Fiona Radman, and Sanja

Plavljanic-Sirola) for your support, belief, and eternal encouragement. And to Robyn Silverton for our Spirited partnership.

To the entire team at Hay House UK, particularly Michelle Pilley. Thank you for welcoming me into the Hay House family and giving my work a home.

To my commissioning editor and friend, Amy Kiberd. Thank you for holding such a crystal clear vision for these pages and making the process such a sacred joy. I'm so proud of this co-creation!

To Julie Oughton and Sandy Draper for polishing this manuscript with a powerful mix of love and extreme attention to detail. To Jo Burgess, Ruth Tewkesbury, Jessica Crockett, Tom Cole, Leanne Siu Anastasi, and Diane Hill for always going beyond and being so supportive and skillful. It's a dream come true to work with each of you.

To Reid Tracy, Patty Gift, the team at Hay House USA, The Writer's Workshop, and to Leon Nacson and Rosie Barry at Hay House Australia, for giving *Light Is the New Black* wings. To Versha Jones (UK) and Michelle Polizzi (USA) for the beautiful cover designs.

To Louise Hay, Maya Angelou, and all of the women from all of the ages who have courageously risen before, regardless of the repercussions. Thank you for blazing such an epic trail and making it safer than ever for women like me to share what's in our souls.

To the Councils of Light, Divine Mother, Kali, Mary Magdalene, my spirit guides, ancestors, and Source. Thank you for your constant whispers, guidance, and support throughout my life, especially in the moments that I ignored it.

To all of my clients, students, and social media followers, thank you for showing up and letting me share what is in my heart.

And finally, but most importantly to you, dear reader. Thank you for answering my call and being so willing to shine your light. You are my blessing.

Love,

Rebecca x

ABOUT THE AUTHOR

Jamie Beadon

Rebecca Campbell is an author, inspirational motivational speaker, spiritual teacher, grounded intuitive mentor, and practical intuitive guide.

One of Hay House's freshest voices, Rebecca is passionate about helping people connect with their intuition in order to live wonderful lives both personally and professionally.

Drawing on her unique experience as an award-winning advertising creative director, Rebecca also guides her clients and students to light up the world with their authentic presence, to 'Let your spirit be your brand™'.

Co-creator of The Spirited Project, she teaches regularly and has been featured in several publications such as *The Sunday Times Style* magazine and *Psychologies*.

As a twentysomething jet-setter meets gypsy spirit, Rebecca blogged her way around the world as The Skype Nomad and shared her adventures in a regular column in *The Daily Telegraph*. She also spent a year of her life painting her way around the world with the Let's Colour Project.

Originally from the sunny shores of Sydney, Rebecca now lives in London but you can find her down under most summers getting her salt water and sunshine fix.

 /rebeccathoughts   @rebeccathoughts

www.rebeccacampbell.me
www.thespiritedproject.com

HAY HOUSE

Look within

Join the conversation about latest products,
events, exclusive offers and more.

f Hay House UK

🐦 @HayHouseUK

📷 @hayhouseuk

💜 healyourlife.com

We'd love to hear from you!